DISCOVER A TRUE HIGHLANDS AND ISLAND

THE

HIGHLANDS

AND

ISLANDS

OF

SCOTLAND

HOLIDAY IDEAS FOR THE SPRING AND SUMMER 1993

Highlands & Islands
OF SCOTLAND.

There's no place like The Highlands and Islands of Scotland in Spring and Summer. It's a land steeped in history and rich with visual splendour.

Whole hillsides burst into bright colours. Long golden sunsets go right on till dawn. And to cap it all, there's our legendary Highland hospitality.

It's a land you'll find easy to discover, too, thanks to our 148 page Spring/ Summer brochure.

It's packed with holiday ideas, from strenuous activity holidays to quiet breaks, just unwinding and doing nothing.

So come and enjoy a holiday you'll never forget - in the Highlands and Islands of Scotland.

For your free colour brochure, call free on 0800 838 166. Or write to: Highlands and Islands of Scotland, Freepost (AD5), Inverness, IV1 1BY, Scotland.

Highlands & Islands
OF SCOTLAND

SELF-CATERING

COUR KINTYRE

Cour is a private estate on the east coast of Kintyre, nine miles north of Carradale, remote, but not isolated.

Two houses, one annexe and four cottages, formerly the homes of estate workers, accommodating from two to twelve, all electric, well equipped, cots, launderette at farm.

Private beach, boats, good sea fishing. Trout fishing in three hill lochs, badminton and ping-pong, all at no extra charge.

The area is a naturalists' paradise and is ideal for hill walking. Many places of interest within a day's drive. Ferries to the islands.

Car essential, parking. Shopping at Carradale or Skipness. Pets accepted.

SAE for brochure to:

Mrs Nickerson, Cour, by Campbeltown, Argyll PA28 6QL
Tel: Skipness (08806) 236; if no reply ring (08806) 233 (Farm).

SELF-CATERING/CARAVANS

APPIN HOLIDAY HOMES
IN A NATURALISTS' PARADISE

CHALETS   COTTAGES   CARAVANS

Holiday Homes in a magical setting mid-way OBAN-FORT WILLIAM.
Ten chalet-bungalows, three traditional cottages, eight modern caravans
right on lochside. All fully serviced and equipped. Sleep 2-5.

Midway	Excellent	STB
Oban –	Touring	♛♛♛♛
Fort William	Centre	Commended

IDEAL FOR FAMILIES . . . ALSO HONEYMOONS!

FREE FISHING (salt and freshwater). Boating, sailing and great hill walks. Pony
trekking and Licensed Inn nearby. Lots to do and see.

PLAY AREA   RECREATION ROOM   LAUNDERETTE   BABY SITTING

Special Spring, Autumn and Winter Terms.

Please send SAE for colour brochure giving dates required.

OPEN ALL YEAR

Price guide . . . £135-£345 per unit weekly

Mr and Mrs F.G. Weir
Appin Holiday Homes
Appin, Argyll PA38 4BQ
Tel: Appin 287 (0631 73287)

Duntrune Castle
Crinan, Argyll

**Stonebuilt character cottages for self-catering
holidays in peaceful comfort.**

Renowned for its historical interest, wildlife and outstanding scenery,
Loch Crinan provides an ideal setting for a peaceful holiday without
being too remote.

These traditional stone-built cottages on a 5,000 acre estate along its
shores, have their own individual character and private garden. All
are recently modernised, attractively furnished, fully equipped, with
wood-burning stoves or open fires, fridges, spin driers, tumble driers
and duvets; home-cooked meals are also available on the premises.

Sleeping accommodation varies from three to five persons.

Much of the estate is designated by the Scottish Natural Heritage, and
noted for its archaeological sites. Hill walking, bird watching and
fishing abound and other activities nearby include pony trekking,
golf, boating and water sports. Good centre for visiting the islands and
there are excellent eating-out places locally.

SAE requested, or telephone for further details to:
SUSAN MALCOLM, DUNTRUNE CASTLE,
KILMARTIN, ARGYLL PA31 8QQ
Telephone: 054-65-283

The Highland Estate of Ellary and Castle Swe

OFFERS

* PEACE

* SECLUSION

* VARIETY OF
  INTERESTS

* FREEDOM

* HISTORY

* OUTSTANDING
  SCENERY

SELF-CATERING/CARAVANS

This 15,000-acres Highland Estate lies in one of the most beautiful and unspoilt areas of Scotland and has a wealth of ancient historical associations within its bounds. There is St. Columba's Cave, probably one of the first places of Christian worship in Britain, also Castle Sween, the oldest ruined castle in Scotland, and Kilmory Chapel where there is a fascinating collection of Celtic slabs.

There is a wide range of accommodation, from small groups of cottages, many of the traditional stone-built estate type to modern holiday chalets, super luxury and luxury caravans at Castle Sween.

Most of the cottages accommodate up to six, but one will take eight. All units fully equipped except linen. Television reception is included in all but one cottage, where reception is not possible. Ellary is beautiful at all times of the year and offers windsurfing, fishing, swimming, sailing and the observation of a wide variety of wildlife; paths and tracks have been marked and signposted throughout the estate as an encouragement to the visitor who prefers to explore on foot, and guests will find farmers and estate workers most helpful in their approach.

For further details, brochure and booking forms, please apply to:
ELLARY ESTATE OFFICE by LOCHGILPHEAD, ARGYLL.
Ormsary (088-03) 232/209 or Achnamara (054-685) 223.

SELF-CATERING

Mr & Mrs E. Crawford, Blarghour Farm, Lochaweside, by Dalmally, Argyll PA33 1BW
Tel: Kilchrenan (086-63) 246

Loch Awe is a very lovely inland loch some 25 miles long with Blarghour Farm situated mid-way along its Eastern shore.

A choice of four magnificently situated holiday homes accommodating from 2 to 8 persons afford panoramic vistas of loch and mountain in an atmosphere of peaceful serenity.

Comfort is assured by central heating, double glazing, tasteful decoration and furnishing, telephone and colour TV, while fitted kitchens, well appointed to include fridge/freezers and washer/dryers, ensure convenience.

Scenic area for touring and walking. Beautiful gardens and historic castles to visit. Bird-watching, boating and fishing to enjoy. Open all year. Regret no pets.

Illustrated brochure gladly sent on request.

🌷🌷🌷🌷 **DE LUXE**   🌷🌷🌷🌷🌷 **HIGHLY COMMENDED**

Idyllic situation in Glen Lonan – Taynuilt 1 mile, Oban 12 miles

Spacious holiday flats with 1, 2, or 3 bedrooms etc. Also small Chalet (sleeps 2 only).
Extensive grounds facing Ben Cruachan, secluded and quiet.
Excellent centre for touring with much to do and see in the area.
Open April to October. Prices from £105 to £370 inclusive of VAT. Electricity extra.
* Colour TV *Initial food delivery service *Linen hire.
Write or telephone Mr and Miss Grant for full details in a colour brochure.

LONAN HOUSE, TAYNUILT, ARGYLL PA35 1HY   TEL: 08662 253

Scottish Tourist Board
COMMENDED
Facilities

MID-ARGYLL. Comfortable converted farm building.
Sleeps 2-6, weekly prices £60-£230. Sorry no dogs.

**SAE to Mike Murray, Kilmahumaig, Crinan, Lochgilphead,
Argyll PA31 8SW. Tel. Crinan (054-683) 238.**

(see line entries)   S.T.B. ♛♛♛ COMMENDED

ARGYLL

LAG-NA-KEIL CHALETS, Lerags, Oban, Argyll PA34 4SE
Telephone (0631) 62746

Lag-na-Keil offers peace and quiet in Lerags Glen, 3½ miles south of Oban on a seven acre wooded site with scenic views. One, two or three bedroomed bungalows or chalets. Fully equipped, except linen, including colour TV. Ideal centre for Islands and Highlands. Free fishing. 14 foot 25 H.P. boat for hire. Laundrette and public telephone on site. Pets welcome. Up to 🥇🥇🥇 commended.
For brochure write (enclosing S.A.E.) or phone John and Fiona Turnbull.

BARMOLLOCH COTTAGES

Peacefully situated midway along the scenic Kilmichael Glen on a steading which was a way station during the great cattle droves from the Highlands and Islands. Three cottages, each sleeping 6, with colour TV, electric central heating, washing machine/tumble dryer, fridge/freezer, microwave and dishwasher. All linen provided. Boat with engine, and fishing equipment available. Mountain bikes for hire. One small dog welcome by arrangement. Ideal area for walking, cycling, fishing, riding and touring. No smoking in the cottages. For brochure please write enclosing SAE or telephone:
Iain & Wendy McCutcheon, Barmolloch Farm, Kilmichael Glen, Lochgilphead, Argyll PA31 8RJ   Telephone: Ford (054-681) 209

KNOCK COTTAGE
Lochgair, Lochgilphead, Argyll PA31 8RZ
Tel: Minard (0546) 86331

Superbly situated in 10 acres of beautiful, wild garden, loch and field, with glorious views over Lochgair and Loch Fyne, Knock Cottage, an ancient croft with modern, comfortable additions is an ideal base for exploring Mid-Argyll with its famous gardens, castles, and breath-taking scenery. In Spring only an hour and a half from Glencoe skiing. On the route to Islay and Jura. Two bedrooms with good views are available, one Double, one Twin, each with private facilities. A beautiful drawing-room and a characterful dining-room also at our guests' disposal.

Bed and Breakfast from £15; Dinner £14.50   S.A.E. for brochure and booking form to Mr & Mrs Mark Reynolds

---

When making enquiries please mention FHG Publications.

Please remember a stamped addressed envelope with enquiries.

FOR THE MUTUAL GUIDANCE OF GUEST AND HOST

Every year literally thousands of holidays, short-breaks and overnight stops are arranged through our guides, the vast majority without any problems at all. In a handful of cases, however, difficulties do arise about bookings, which often could have been prevented from the outset.

It is important to remember that when accommodation has been booked, both parties — guests and hosts — have entered into a form of contract. We hope that the following points will provide helpful guidance.

GUESTS: When enquiring about accommodation, be as precise as possible. Give exact dates, numbers in your party and the ages of any children. State the number and type of rooms wanted and also what catering you require — bed and breakfast, full board, etc. Make sure that the position about evening meals is clear — and about pets, reductions for children or any other special points.

Read our reviews carefully to ensure that the proprietors you are going to contact can supply what you want. Ask for a letter confirming all arrangements, if possible.

If you have to cancel, do so as soon as possible. Proprietors do have the right to retain deposits and under certain circumstances to charge for cancelled holidays if adequate notice is not given and they cannot re-let the accommodation.

HOSTS: Give details about your facilities and about any special conditions. Explain your deposit system clearly and arrangements for cancellations, charges, etc, and whether or not your terms include VAT.

If for any reason you are unable to fulfil an agreed booking without adequate notice, you may be under an obligation to arrange alternative suitable accommodation or to make some form of compensation.

While every effort is made to ensure accuracy, we regret that FHG Publications cannot accept responsibility for errors, omissions or misrepresentation in our entries or any consequences thereof. Prices in particular should be checked because we go to press early. We will follow up complaints but cannot act as arbiters or agents for either party.

GLEN NEVIS

Holiday Cottages

**Glen Nevis, Fort William
Inverness-shire PH33 6SX
For brochure write, or telephone
(0397) 702191**

🌹🌹🌹 Commended

For your Scottish Holiday hire a luxury holiday home in picturesque Glen Nevis. Our modern self-contained cottages are fully equipped for 2-5 people and have an idyllic Highland situation only 2.5 miles from Fort William. Fully heated and insulated, very comfortable with big reductions for out-of-season holidays!

GLEN NEVIS

Holiday Caravans

**Glen Nevis, Fort William
Inverness-shire PH33 6SX
For brochure write, or telephone
(0397) 702191**

Thistle Award

Hire a luxury 4-6 berth Caravan in the heart of the romantic Western Highlands close to mighty Ben Nevis. All caravans are completely self-contained having hot and cold water, shower, toilet, colour television, refrigerator, etc.

ACHNABOBANE FARMHOUSE

By Spean Bridge, Fort William
Telephone: 039-781 342

Ideally situated for hill walking, fishing, shooting or touring, the south-facing Achnabobane Farmhouse, set amidst a 100-acre working farm with a herd of Highland cattle, is on the main A82 road overlooking Ben Nevis and the new Aonach Mhor Ski Slope. The comfortable bedrooms all have wash-basins and kettles for evening "cuppas". Children welcome. Bed and Breakfast from £13; Dinner, Bed and Breakfast from £21. Open all year round.

ROYBRIDGE – *NA TIGHEAN BEAGA*
East Park, Roy Bridge, Inverness-shire PH31 4AG

STB Commended 2-4 Crowns   **Mr F.S. Matheson**   **Tel. Spean Bridge (039781) 370/436**

A small private development of bungalows and chalets. Fort William 12 miles. Close to Rivers Spean and Roy with splendid views over Glen Spean and Ben Nevis mountain range. Ideal for climbing, walking, fishing. The units are well-appointed and furnished, with bed linen, except towels. Quality homes for 2/8 persons, each is self-contained, all-electric, fully carpeted, colour TV, 2/4 bedrooms, sittingroom with bed settee, dinette with cooker, fridge, modern units. Bathrooms have bath or shower, some both. Heating all rooms. Laundry with washing machine, etc. Metered electricity. Shop 300 yards. Parking. Pets welcome. Member BH&HPA and ASSC. Weekly terms £125 to £440 (inc. VAT). SAE for further details.

ARDGARRY FARM

Faichem, Invergarry, Inverness-shire. Tel. Invergarry (080 93) 226

Try a relaxing holiday on a small working farm in a traditional Scottish farmhouse and lodge. (Plenty of animals and a children's pony). Good home cooking, cosy bedrooms, comfortable lounge/diningroom with panoramic views across the Glen to Ben Tee (2,950ft.) Ideally situated for exploring the Highland Region, either by car or on foot. Good fishing, beautiful forest walks. Visit Loch Ness, Skye, Aviemore and the lovely Glen Garry. Substantial Dinner, Bed and Breakfast £17.50 per person per day. All rooms have hot/cold running water. Tea/coffee making facilities. Central heating, ample parking.

Self Catering also available.
Proprietors Mr and Mrs Roy Wilson.

Torguish House Daviot, Inverness. Tel: 0463 772208

The world famous author of 'HMS Ulysses' and 'The Guns of Navarone' and 17 other major novels which enthral millions, spent his formative childhood years in Torguish House. Once the local manse it is now an extremely homely Guest House offering nine bedrooms, four having ensuite facilities. Welcoming log fire with big accommodating armchairs are in the TV lounge. Children welcome; adventure play area. Ideal touring centre and golf and fishing are nearby. Detailed brochure available on request. B&B £11; D,B&B £18. Ensuite B&B £15; Ensuite D,B&B £22. Children under 2 years free; 2-8 years B&B from £7; over 8 years ensuite £11. ♥♥♥ Commended.

DIRECTIONS: **From the North** on the A9, 4 miles south of Inverness, Torguish is 150 yards on the **LEFT** past the sign for Croy and Culloden. **From the South** on the A9, move into the right lane after passing the Daviot East junction (B9154). Access to Torguish approx. 200 yards on the **RIGHT** across central reservation.

INVERNESS-SHIRE

REELIG GLEN HOLIDAY COTTAGES & CHALETS

In the Scottish Highlands near Inverness

🏵🏵 Approved up to 🏵🏵🏵🏵 Commended

Holiday cottages with character and cedarwood chalets set individually among the trees or fields of a beautiful old Highland estate. They all have colour television, electric fires, night storage and electric water heating and adjoining car parking space. The cottages also have open fires. The countryside with all the untrammelled joys of nature is at the door – butterflies find what butterflies need. Nearby is the Forestry Commission's Forest Walk which is rather special with some of the tallest trees in Britain. Reelig is an excellent central base from which to see all parts of the Highlands. Fishing, pony trekking and dozens of interests are available locally. Rates are reduced in spring and autumn. ASSC Member.

Brochure available from Malcolm Fraser (FHG), Reelig Glen Estate, Kirkhill, Inverness-shire. Telephone 046-383 208 (24 hours)

BOARD

ARDMUIR HOUSE

🏵🏵🏵 Commended   Les Routiers   AA **QQQ**

Situated beside the River Ness, this family-run hotel close to the town centre and Ness Islands offers the ideal base for touring the Highlands.

All bedrooms have en-suite facilities, hair driers, colour TV and tea-making.

Our non-smoking dining room, with benefit of a residents' licence, offers home cooking with fresh local produce.

Terms: Dinner, Bed and Breakfast from £32 per day. Brochure and tariff, with discounts for stays of 3 days or more from:

Jean and Tony Gatcombe, Ardmuir House, 16 Ness Bank, Inverness IV2 4SF Telephone: 0463 231151

SELF-CATERING

SELF-CATERING HOLIDAY COTTAGES

Situated in the village of Foyers, 19 miles south of Inverness on the B852 which overlooks Loch Ness, two semi-detached cottages for holiday letting. The accommodation, suitable for up to five guests, consists of two bedrooms, one double and one with a double and single bed; lounge. The kitchen/dining area is fully equipped with cooker, refrigerator and usual utensils, crockery and cutlery for five. Instant hot water heaters, convector heaters and television; electricity by 50p slot meter. There are excellent opportunities for outdoor recreation with hill walking, river and loch fishing, nature trails amidst beautiful mountain scenery, and of course "Monster Spotting". There is a pleasant garden for relaxing in. Car parking adjacent to both properties.

Also 2 self-catering cottages in Inverness.

PATMAC HOLIDAY ENTERPRISES, 103 Church Street, Inverness IV1 1ES. Telephone: 0463 713702

BOARD

Cuilcheanna House Hotel
LICENSED

Cuilcheanna House is peacefully situated in its own grounds just off the main A82 road in the village of Onich. We offer our guests a combination of modern amenities and old fashioned hospitality. All our bedrooms have en-suite facilities and tea making facilities. The dining-room has wonderful views down Loch Linnhe and our food is traditionally prepared using fresh produce.

Dinner, Bed and Breakfast £30-£35 nightly.

Please write for brochure:

Mr & Mrs A. Dewar, Cuilcheanna House, Onich, Fort William, Inverness-shire PH33 6SD. Tel: Onich (08553) 226.

Please mention Farm Guide Scotland when enquiring

Mrs C. M. KILPATRICK   ♛♛/♛♛♛ Commended

Slipperfield House, West Linton, Peeblesshire EH46 7AA (West Linton [0968] 60401)

Two Commended cottages a mile from West Linton at the foot of the Pentland Hills, set in 100 acres of lochs and woodlands. **AMERICA COTTAGE**, which sleeps 6 people in 3 bedrooms, is secluded and has recently been completely modernised. **LOCH COTTAGE**, which sleeps 4 people in 2 bedrooms, is attached to the owner's house and has magnificent views over a seven-acre loch. Both cottages have sitting-rooms with dining areas and colour TV; modern bathrooms and excellently equipped Schreiber kitchens. America Cottage also has washing and drying machines, microwave oven and telephone. Controlled pets allowed. Ample parking; car essential; Edinburgh 19 miles. Golf and private fishing. Available all year. SAE please for terms.

COUNTRY COTTAGES ON DUNALASTAIR HIGHLAND ESTATE

Up to ♛♛♛♛ Commended

The cottages are situated amongst and with views of some of the most beautiful scenery in Scotland. Ideal for hill walking, climbing and bird watching. Golf within half an hour. Excellent brown trout fishing, use of boats rent free. Accommodation for 4-8, all electric and open fire in livingroom. Off-peak heating Spring/Autumn. Dunalastair is a National Scenic Area and in a perfect central position from which to tour Scotland. £126 to £370, inc. VAT, weekly. March to November. Weekends negotiable.

Large SAE please to:
Mrs M. A. MacIntyre, Dunalastair Holiday Houses,
1 Riverside, Tummel Bridge, Pitlochry,
Perthshire PH16 5SB   Tel: (0882) 634285.

STRATHEARN *Holidays*

. . . in the very heart of Scotland. A superb range of vacations based on exclusive developments of luxurious cottages and houses in the very centre of historic and romantic Scotland.

Sport and leisure holidays – golf; shooting; fishing; walking; watersports. Equestrian holidays – with use of all the superb facilities of the Hilton House Stud. Relaxation holidays – the romance of Scotland, castles, palaces and historic houses – discovered through easy access to the Highlands or to Edinburgh and Glasgow. Superb restaurants.

There are no hidden charges; electricity, unlimited hot water, bed linen, etc, are all included in our price. That's great value! To obtain our 12 page colour brochure about our memorable holidays apply (no stamp required) to:

Mr H. England, Strathearn Holidays, Dept. F93, Freepost, Kilda Way, Muirton Industrial Estate, Perth PH1 3RL. Tel: Office 0738 33322 or evening 0738 840263.   ♛♛♛♛ Highly Commended

SELF-CATERING

CLACHAN FARM
Loch Broom, Ullapool,
Ross-shire IV23 2RZ

Come and relax amidst the tranquillity of Loch Broom in two modern three-bedroomed croft bungalows. They are set in an elevated position overlooking Loch Broom, 12 miles from Ullapool and 50 miles north of Inverness. Fully equipped kitchens and very comfortably furnished, they are all-electric with card meter. The comfort of guests is our main priority. Central for touring. In easy reach of Corrieshalloch Gorge, Inverewe Botanical Gardens, Achiltibuie Hydroponicum and Knockan Nature Reserve. Linen extra if required. No smoking. No Sunday enquiries, please. **Apply Mrs Isobel Renwick: Telephone: 0854 85 209** 👑👑 **Commended**

SELF-CATERING

CONIFERS LEISURE PARK, NEWTON STEWART
DUMFRIES & GALLOWAY DG8 6AN

FREE: Over one mile of salmon and sea trout fishing to our guests.

FREE: Golf (ideal for a visit to Turnberry).

29 Scandinavian self-catering luxury chalets, colour TV, sleep 4/6, all electric, double glazed and fully insulated, furnished to high standards. Set in 25 acres of picturesque forest setting.

For the sportsman, river, loch and sea angling, riding, shooting, all within easy reach. A golf course adjacent. Two saunas, Champney health spa, solarium/sun beds. Heated swimming pool, tennis court and barbecue area on site.

Spend an active or relaxing time at Conifers, at any time of the year and you are sure to enjoy yourself.

Lots of places to wine and dine within one mile radius.

Telephone (0671) 2107 or write for brochure.

Please note all advertisers in this colour section also have a full review in the classified section under the relevant county.

The 46th Farm Holiday Guide to
HOLIDAYS
IN
SCOTLAND

Farms, guest houses and country hotels.
Cottages, flats and chalets.
Caravans and camping.
Activity.

FHG

Other FHG Publications

Recommended Short Break Holidays
Recommended Country Hotels of Britain
Recommended Wayside Inns of Britain
Pets Welcome!
Bed and Breakfast in Britain
The Golf Guide: Where to Play/Where to Stay
London's Best Bed and Breakfast Hotels
Farm Holiday Guide England, Wales, Ireland & Channel Islands
Self-Catering & Furnished Holidays
Britain's Best Holidays
Guide to Caravan and Camping Holidays
Bed and Breakfast Stops
Children Welcome! Family Holiday Guide

ISBN 1 85055 155 3 © FHG Publications Ltd.
Cover photograph: Inveraray, Loch Fyne, by Still Moving Picture Co.
Design by Edward Carden (Glasgow).

Typeset by R.D. Composition Ltd., Glasgow.
Printed and bound by Benham's Ltd., Colchester.

Distribution – **Book Trade**: WLM, 117 The Hollow, Littleover, Derby DE3 7BS (Tel: 0332 272020. Fax: 0332 774287).
News Trade: UMD, 1 Benwell Road, Holloway, London N7 7AX (Tel: 071-700 4600. Fax: 071-607 3352).

Published by FHG Publications Ltd.,
Abbey Mill Business Centre, Seedhill, Paisley PA1 1TJ (041-887 0428).
A member of the U.N. Group.

———

US ISBN 1-55650-543-4
Distributed in the United States by
Hunter Publishing Inc., 300 Raritan Center Parkway CN94,
Edison, N.J., 08818, USA

CONTENTS

Full Colour Section 1 – 16
(Start of Book)

FHG

THE FHG DIPLOMA

HELP IMPROVE
BRITISH TOURIST STANDARDS

You are choosing holiday accommodation from our very popular FHG Publications. Whether it be a hotel, guest house, farmhouse or self-catering accommodation, we think you will find it hospitable, comfortable and clean, and your host and hostess friendly and helpful.

Why not write and tell us about it?

As a recognition of the generally well-run and excellent holiday accommodation reviewed in our publications, we at FHG Publications Ltd. present a diploma to proprietors who receive the highest recommendation from their guests who are also readers of our Guides. If you care to write to us praising the holiday you have booked through FHG Publications Ltd. – whether this be board, self-catering accommodation, a sporting or a caravan holiday, what you say will be evaluated and the proprietors who reach our final list will be contacted.

The winning proprietor will receive an attractive framed diploma to display on his premises as recognition of a high standard of comfort, amenity and hospitality. FHG Publications Ltd. offer this diploma as a contribution towards the improvement of standards in tourist accommodation in Britain. Help your excellent host or hostess to win it!

FHG DIPLOMA

We nominate ....

....

Because

Name ....

Address ....

.... Telephone No. ....

FOREWORD

The Farm Holiday Guide to

Holidays in

SCOTLAND

1993

You will enjoy the entries in this new edition of *Farm Holiday Guide*, now in its 46th year. Holidays in the country and in quiet coastal resorts remain excellent value and standards of accommodation and service have risen greatly over the years.

"Clean, comfortable accommodation; wholesome and well-cooked food (where applicable) and a courteous welcome" have been our requirement of advertisers since *Farm Holiday Guide* first promoted rural holidays. The National Touist Boards and other organisations such as the Countryside Commission have more recently helped to encourage and define objective standards and we are very pleased that "Crowns" and "Keys" figure prominently in our latest edition as does our own category of "Working Farms".

The *Farm Holiday Guide* offers you all the freedom and economy of making your own holiday arrangements directly with proprietors or managers and not through a bureau or agency. To make the most of these benefits you may find the following points helpful.

ENQUIRIES AND BOOKINGS. Give full details of dates (with an alternative), numbers and any special requirements. Ask about any points in the holiday description which are not clear and make sure that prices and conditions are clearly explained. You should receive confirmation in writing and a receipt for any deposit or advance payment. If you book your holiday well in advance, especially self-catering, confirm your arrival details nearer the time. Some proprietors, especially for self-catering, request full payment in advance but a reasonable deposit is more normal.

CANCELLATIONS. A holiday booking is a form of contract with obligations on both sides. If you have to cancel, give as much notice as possible. The longer the notice the better the chance that your host can replace your booking and therefore refund any payments. If the proprietor cancels in such a way that causes serious inconvenience, he may have obligations to you which have not been properly honoured. Take advice if necessary from such organisations as the Citizen's Advice Bureau, Consumer's Association, Trading Standards Office, Local Tourist Office, etc., or your own solicitor.

COMPLAINTS. It's best if any problems can be sorted out at the start of your holiday. If the problem is not solved, you can contact the organisations mentioned above. You can also write to us. We will follow up the complaint with the advertiser – but we cannot act as intermediaries or accept responsibility for holiday arrangements.

FHG Publications Ltd. do not inspect accommodation and an entry in our guides does not imply a recommendation. However our advertisers have signed their agreement to work for the holidaymaker's best interests and as their customer, you have the right to expect appropriate attention and service.

HOLIDAY INSURANCE. It is possible to insure against holiday cancellation. Brokers and insurance companies can advise you about this.

We hope that *Farm Holiday Guide 1993* will bring you many happy holidays. Don't forget our **Farm Holiday Guide Diploma**. Every year we award a small number of Diplomas to holiday proprietors who have been specially recommended to us by readers. Your hosts will appreciate your recommendation and we are always pleased to hear from you.

You will find the list of **Farm Holiday Guide Diploma** winners for 1992 included on page 31. We'd welcome your suggestions for 1993!

We would also appreciate your mention *Farm Holiday Guide* whenever you make an enquiry or booking.

Peter Clark
Publishing Director

SCOTLAND

TOWNS AND
MAIN ROADS

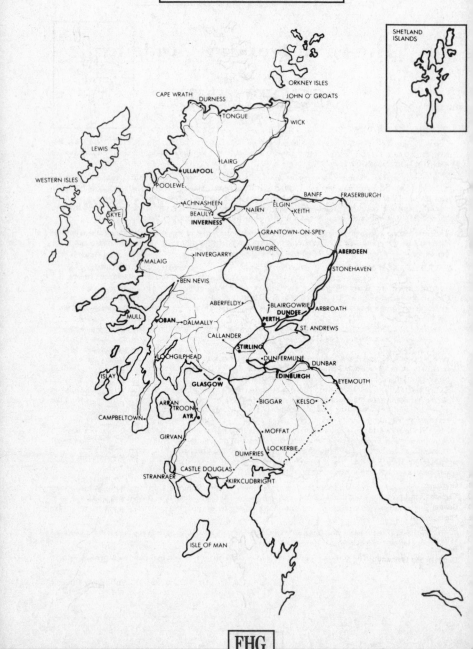

SHETLAND
ISLANDS

ORKNEY ISLES

CAPE WRATH
DURNESS
JOHN O' GROATS
TONGUE
WICK

LEWIS

LAIRG

WESTERN ISLES
ULLAPOOL

POOLEWE
BANFF
FRASERBURGH
ACHNASHEEN
ELGIN
NAIRN
KEITH
SKYE
BEAULY
INVERNESS
GRANTOWN-ON-SPEY

INVERGARRY
AVIEMORE
ABERDEEN
MALAIG
STONEHAVEN
BEN NEVIS

ABERFELDY
MULL
BLAIRGOWRIE
ARBROATH
OBAN
DALMALLY
DUNDEE
PERTH
CALLANDER
ST. ANDREWS
STIRLING
LOCHGILPHEAD
DUNFERMLINE
DUNBAR
ISLAY
GLASGOW
EDINBURGH
EYEMOUTH
BIGGAR
KELSO
ARRAN
TROON
CAMPBELTOWN
AYR
MOFFAT
GIRVAN
LOCKERBIE
DUMFRIES
CASTLE DOUGLAS
STRANRAER
KIRKCUDBRIGHT

ISLE OF MAN

FHG

SCOTLAND
COUNTIES
AND REGIONS

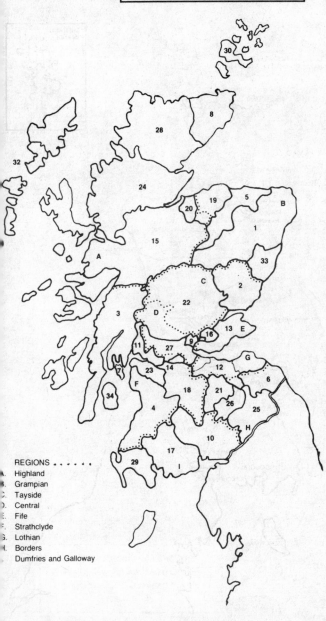

SCOTLAND
1. Aberdeenshire
2. Angus
3. Argyll
4. Ayrshire
5. Banffshire
6. Berwickshire
7. Bute
8. Caithness
9. Clackmannanshire
10. Dumfriesshire
11. Dunbartonshire
12. Edinburgh
   and the Lothians
13. Fife
14. Glasgow
15. Inverness-shire
16. Kinross-shire
17. Kirkcudbrightshire
18. Lanarkshire
19. Morayshire
20. Nairnshire
21. Peeblesshire
22. Perthshire
23. Renfrewshire
24. Ross-shire
25. Roxburghshire
26. Selkirkshire
27. Stirlingshire
28. Sutherland
29. Wigtownshire
30. Orkney
31. Shetlands
32. Western Isles
33. Kincardine
34. Arran

REGIONS . . . . . .
A. Highland
B. Grampian
C. Tayside
D. Central
E. Fife
F. Strathclyde
G. Lothian
H. Borders
    Dumfries and Galloway

Beautiful monument to Robert Burns which stands in gardens on the banks of the River Doon at Alloway.

ABERDEENSHIRE

BALLATER. Maria and Michael Franklin, Netherley Guest House, 2 Netherley Place, Ballater AB35

5QE (Ballater [03397] 55792). 🐾🐾 *Commended.* Ballater is a pretty town, close to Balmoral Castle, ideally placed for touring beautiful Royal Deeside and the Grampians. It is a good base for walking, climbing, angling, golf, gliding etc. The famous Castle and Whisky Trails are nearby. It offers good access to both Glenshee and Lecht ski slopes (30 minutes). Located by the Village Green, the Netherley is a family-run guest house offering a very friendly, comfortable stay and good cooking. AA Listed. Nine bedrooms, some with en-suite facilities. TV lounge. Bed and Breakfast £14 to £19. Evening Meals available.

HUNTLY. Mrs Ingram, Bogton, Fogue, Huntly AB54 6HN (04647 237). Working farm. A warm welcome awaits you at comfortably homely farmhouse on family run farm, in peaceful surroundings, seven miles from Huntly, 20 miles from coast. Ideal area for touring, Castle Trails, Whisky Trails, golf courses and pony trekking. Accommodation for guests in one double bedroom and one twin bedroom (cot available), bathroom, sitting/diningroom. Traditional Scottish food. Car essential. No pets. Open March to October for one night, one week or a weekend break. Evening cuppa and home bakes. Bed and Breakfast £11; Evening Meal on request £5.

INVERURIE. Mrs E.A. Thorp, Meikle Pitinnan, Wartle, Inverurie AB51 0EH (04675 276). 🐾🐾 *Commended.* **Working farm, join in.** Built in 1835 Meikle Pitinnan, formerly a staging post and inn, is now a comfortable and recently modernised farmhouse. We offer good home cooking and comforts with "join in" activities. Situated on Castle trail and Whisky trail, beautiful walks around Benachie with Royal Deeside on our doorstep. Coast with sandy beaches within easy reach and Aviemore one hour's drive away. Shops, post office and public houses in local village. Family or double room, bathroom en-suite; bathroom with shaver point and shower; central heating; colour TV; sittingroom and separate diningroom. Parking. Sorry, no pets. Children welcome. Bed and Breakfast from £14; Evening Meal available. SAE for terms.

OLD MELDRUM. Mrs Elizabeth I. Shewan, Springbank, Distillery Road, Old Meldrum AB51 0ES (06512 2431). Situated in a quiet street off main Aberdeen/Banff road (A947). Accommodation offered in one large comfortable twin room with sofa bed in room. Central heating, colour TV, tea/coffee making facilities. In centre of Castle Trail, within walking distance of 18 hole golf course and bowling green. Very good eating places in village. In easy reach of hill walks, beaches and the city of Aberdeen. Bed and Breakfast from £12.50 to £14. Good food.

ANGUS

BRECHIN by. Jean Stewart, Wood of Auldbar, Aberlemno, By Brechin DD9 6SZ (030 783 218).

Wood of Auldbar is a family farm of 187 acres with lovely farmhouse in first class condition. Very central for touring the Angus Glens, Royal Deeside, Balmoral, Glamis plus many more castles within easy reach. Beaches, nature walks, birdwatching, fishing, golf and leisure facilities all near at hand. Standing Stones and lovely churches. Family, twin and single rooms. Lounge. Excellent farmhouse cooking and baking in award-winning farmhouse. Food Hygiene Certificate held. Children welcome, cot available. Dogs by arrangement. Bed and Breakfast from £12.50; Dinner optional from £7. A warm welcome awaits you.

FORFAR. Mrs Catherine Jolly, West Mains of Turin Farm, Rescobie, By Forfar DD8 2TE (Aberlemno

[030-783] 229 changing in 1993 to 0307 830229). ♛♛ *Commended.* **Working farm, join in.** Our stock rearing farm enjoys panoramic view over Rescobie Loch on the Montrose/Forfar road (B9113). It is an ideal base for exploring places of historic interest (Glamis Castle, the priory at Resterneth, Standing Stones at Aberlemno). There is a lovely walk up to a ruined castle fort in the farm grounds. Golf and fishing nearby. A friendly welcome and lovely atmosphere awaits guests. Home cooking and baking served. Snooker and croquet for evening entertainment. Lovely garden. Ample parking. Full central heating. Comfortable lounge with colour TV and open fire. Evening Meal by arrangement in the diningroom. One family, one double and one single bedroom; bathroom and shower room with toilet. SAE or telephone for further details, please.

FOR THE MUTUAL GUIDANCE
OF GUEST AND HOST

Every year literally thousands of holidays, short-breaks and overnight stops are arranged through our guides, the vast majority without any problems at all. In a handful of cases, however, difficulties do arise about bookings, which often could have been prevented from the outset.

It is important to remember that when accommodation has been booked, both parties — guests and hosts — have entered into a form of contract. We hope that the following points will provide helpful guidance.

GUESTS: When enquiring about accommodation, be as precise as possible. Give exact dates, numbers in your party and the ages of any children. State the number and type of rooms wanted and also what catering you require — bed and breakfast, full board, etc. Make sure that the position about evening meals is clear — and about pets, reductions for children or any other special points.

Read our reviews carefully to ensure that the proprietors you are going to contact can supply what you want. Ask for a letter confirming all arrangements, if possible.

If you have to cancel, do so as soon as possible. Proprietors do have the right to retain deposits and under certain circumstances to charge for cancelled holidays if adequate notice is not given and they cannot re-let the accommodation.

HOSTS: Give details about your facilities and about any special conditions. Explain your deposit system clearly and arrangements for cancellations, charges, etc, and whether or not your terms include VAT.

If for any reason you are unable to fulfil an agreed booking without adequate notice, you may be under an obligation to arrange alternative suitable accommodation or to make some form of compensation.

While every effort is made to ensure accuracy, we regret that FHG Publications cannot accept responsibility for errors, omissions or misrepresentation in our entries or any consequences thereof. Prices in particular should be checked because we go to press early. We will follow up complaints but cannot act as arbiters or agents for either party.

ARGYLL

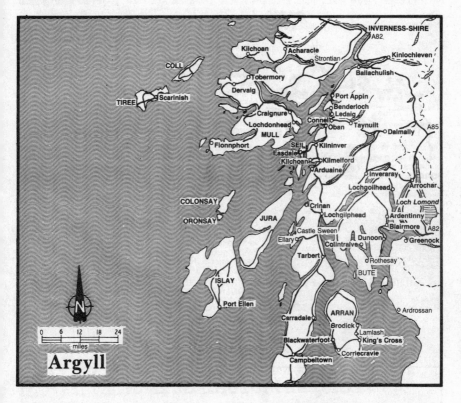

ACHARACLE. The Clan Morrison Hotel, Glenborrodale, Acharacle PH36 4JP (09724 232). Small family-run hotel on the shores of Loch Sunart. All bedrooms have private bathrooms, radio and tea making facilities. Licensed. Diningroom and bar have panoramic views over Loch Sunart. Varied menus offered. Bar lunch and dinner available. The hotel also offers two luxury self catering bungalows sleeping five/seven people. Children and pets welcome. Please write or telephone for terms and further details.

STRATHCLYDE REGION – WHERE TO START?

Scotland's most densely populated region houses more people than many small countries. At its centre is Glasgow where you will find many attractions including the Art Gallery and the Burrell Collection. Heading further out this Region includes such popular places as Oban, the Mull of Kintyre, the Clyde Valley, the Ayrshire Coast and Argyll Forest Park.

ACHARACLE. Fergie MacDonald, Clanranald Hotel Complex, Acharacle, Near Fort William (096 785 662).  This is a modern five bedroomed Highland inn, set in 70 acres of rough sheep farm, with restaurant and bar. All rooms have full private facilities. Salmon and sea trout fishing on Lochshiel, with boats and engines supplied. Also brown trout fishing on hill lochs. Clay pigeon shooting on hotel range and red deer stalking in October. There are also **three self-catering holiday cottages and one caravan available sleeping four/six persons**. Full details on request.

ARDMADDY, by Oban. Mrs D. Gilbert, Ardshellach Farm, Ardmaddy, By Oban PA34 4QY (085 23218). Working beef cattle and sheep farm situated on the Ardmaddy road 12 miles from Oban on the B844 to Easdale and approximately one mile from the Bridge over the Atlantic and Ardmaddy Castle gardens. This quiet accommodation is 400 yards from the sea overlooking Luing and Scarba and comprises one room sleeping two/four. Bathroom with bath and shower adjacent. TV lounge. Bed and Breakfast from £12 includes evening cup of tea.

BALLACHULISH. Mrs M.J. Dow, Tigh Ard, Brecklet, Ballachulish PA39 4JG (085 52 328). Tigh Ard is a most attractively situated bungalow, on a superb elevated site, with magnificent views over the village of Ballachulish and Loch Leven and surrounded by an acre of delightful mature grounds. Ample parking space. Lovely garden. One double and one twin bedrooms; bathroom with bath, washbasin and shower also another toilet with washbasin next door to bedrooms. Central heating, colour TV in sun lounge. There are many lovely walks around the area which is very central for touring the Western Highlands. Bed and Breakfast from £11.50 (bedtime drink included). Tourist Board registered.

BALLACHULISH. Mr and Mrs W. & J. Watson, Craiglinnhe Guest House, Ballachulish PA39 4JX (Ballachulish [08552] 270).  🏵 🏵 🏵 *Commended*. Craiglinnhe, situated close to the water's edge, enjoys spectacular views of loch and mountain. Excellent touring centre for Western Highlands; four miles north of Glencoe on the A828 (Oban road). Wide range of local amenities including walking, sailing, fishing and sites of historical interest. Set in beautiful gardens, this small family-run guest house provides well appointed rooms; four twin, two double, including ground floor accommodation; all rooms have private facilities; tea/coffee making facilities; central heating throughout. Elegant lounge and dining room. Pets by arrangement. Bed and Breakfast from £18 to £21 per person per night; Dinner available. Ample parking. Open December to October. **Brochure on request**.

CARRADALE. Mrs D. MacCormick, Mains Farm, Carradale, Campbeltown PA28 6QG (058-33 216). Working farm. From April to October farmhouse accommodation is offered at Mains Farm, two minutes' walk from safe beach, forestry walks with views of Carradale Bay and Arran. Near main bus route and 15 miles from airport. Golf, sea/river fishing, pony trekking, windsurfing locally. Comfortable accommodation in one double, one single, one family bedrooms; guests' sitting/diningroom with coal/log fire; bathroom, toilet. Heating in rooms according to season. Children welcome at reduced rates, cot, high chair available. Pets by prior arrangement. The house is not suitable for disabled visitors. STB registered. Good home cooking and special diets catered for. Dinner, Bed and Breakfast from £16.50; Bed and Breakfast from £12. Tea and biscuits served late evening.

Peace and Quiet at Rockhill Farm

The Farmhouse

The Farm with Loch Awe & Ben Cruachan

Rockhill is situated on the south-east shore of Loch Awe with panoramic views of the Cruachan range of mountains and Priest Island. Breeding Hanoverian horses, and sheep. 5-Course Dinner, Bed & breakfast, first-class home cooking utilises produce from our large picturesque garden. Though the farmhouse dates back to 1630 it has been attractively modernised with every comfort and convenience. En-suite and private facilities. Five double bedrooms, electric blankets and fires, shaver points, colour TV's, tea & coffee making facilities. Separate diningroom. Lounge overlooking loch. An ideal spot for those who enjoy peace and quiet in beautiful surroundings in a homely family-run Guest House. We have a boat for hire and there are good launching facilities for your own boat. Free trout fishing on Loch Awe. In the area there is abundant wildlife, bird watching, hill walking, pony trekking and horse riding. Places of interest in locality: Inveraray and Kilchurn Castles, Glencoe, Cruachan the hollow mountain and Oban for boat trips to the Isles. Open Easter till end of September. Children over 10 years welcome. Dogs by arrangement. Car essential. AA listed. Fire certificate. Residential licence. Also available two furnished cottages, see under Self-Catering. SAE for comprehensive brochure.

Helen and Brian Whalley, Rockhill Farm Country House, Ardbrecknish, by Dalmally, Argyll PA33 1BH. Telephone 086-63 218.

DUNOON. Mrs M. Kohls, Ashgrove Guest House, Wyndham Road, Innellan, Dunoon PA23 7SH (0369 83306). Ashgrove Guest House in the village of Innellan, four miles south of Dunoon, is ideal for a quiet, restful holiday. In four acres of grounds Ashgrove has ponies, hens, ducks, geese and other small animals. Guests can enjoy leisurely woodland walks, boat or coach trips, or simply relax in the secluded gardens with outstanding views over the Firth of Clyde. For the more energetic visitors golf, tennis, bowls, fishing, pony trekking are all nearby. The shore is only minutes away. Ashgrove is a family-run guest house with a friendly informal atmosphere. Twin, double and family rooms all have en-suite shower, WC and washbasin, colour TV, tea/coffee making facilities. Open all year with mini breaks from October to March. Bed and Breakfast from £14 to £17 daily. Reductions for children and longer stays. Caravan also available; details on request.

FORD. Dr D.W. and Mrs S.W. Bannister, Tigh an Lodan, Ford, By Lochgilphead PA31 8RH (Ford [054681] 287). In scenic seclusion at the southern end of Loch Awe, Ford is three miles south along B840 from A816 Oban road and well situated for the enjoyment of the varied and under-appreciated attractions of mid-Argyll. We offer interesting cuisine in a relaxing environment. Tigh an Lodan has all the modern comforts you expect coupled with pampering touches, such as open fires and plentiful books and magazines in the elegant sittingroom. There is comfortable accommodation for six in well appointed bedrooms served by bathroom, shower room and additional toilet. Only children over 13 years welcome. Pets by arrangement. Terms for Bed and Breakfast from £16; Dinner £10.50. **We are a No Smoking establishment.**

GLENCOE. The Isles of Glencoe Hotel and Leisure Centre, Ballachulish PA39 4HL (08552 603; Fax: 08552 629). The Hotel is set in a Highland estate with two loch-side harbours and three kilometres of water frontage which play host to local craft and watersports. The area is not only a Summer paradise. The famous terrain of Glencoe attracts walkers and climbers year round and in the Winter months the ski resort of Nevis Range combines with Glencoe to make this one of the finest ski centres in Britain. Special offer for 1993! Escape away for any two nights for £39.95 per ROOM per night (subject to availability).

ISLE OF GIGHA. Mrs Margaret McSporran, Post Office Guest House, Isle of Gigha PA41 7AA (058 35 251). A 20 minute sail on a drive-through Caledonian MacBrayne car ferry from Tayinloan on the peninsula of Kintyre in Argyll brings you to this island of unspoiled natural beauty. Here you can relax and enjoy a quiet holiday with beautiful scenery, exotic rhododendron and azalea gardens, sandy beaches, wild birds and flowers and a 9 hole golf course. Bed and Breakfast and Evening Meal. Weekly rates quoted. Excellent home cooking and comfortable accommodation. Washbasins in rooms, TV, tea-making facilities, electric blankets and heaters. Residents' lounge. Also self catering accommodation available.

Sonachan Hotel

Most westerly hotel
on British mainland

The Sonachan Hotel is the most westerly on the British mainland. Three miles from Ardnamurchan Point, set among the hills and quiet countryside in one of the few remaining unspoilt areas of the Scottish Highlands. Car ferry from Mull to Kilchoan. It is a small, comfortable, family-run hotel under the personal supervision of the owners John and Eilidh MacPhail and their daughter Helen who aim to provide maximum comfort in pleasant surroundings with an atmosphere of informality and cheerfulness. *All bedrooms have hot and cold water, shaving points, electric blankets, continental quilts and tea and coffee making facilities. Bed and Breakfast. Terms on request.*

Mr & Mrs J.H. MacPhail, Sonachan Hotel, Kilchoan, Argyll PH36 4LN   Tel: Kilchoan (09723) 211

KILMARTIN. Mrs Joy MacGillivray, Dunchragaig House, By Kilmartin, Lochgilphead PA31 8RG (0546 605209). 🏵🏵 *Commended.* Attractive 19th century house of lovely character, upgraded and finished to a high standard, giving every comfort to our guests. Situated in the heart of Mid-Argyll amidst a conservation area surrounded by historic cairns and henges. It is an ideal centre for touring the West from Campbeltown, Fort William, Oban and also the numerous islands off this coast. A friendly, personal welcome awaits. We offer a varied Scottish breakfast and evening meal and pride ourselves on value for money and excellent service. Bed and Breakfast from £13.50; en-suite rooms available.

KILMARTIN. Mrs C.C. McAuslan, "Cornaig" Guest House, Kilmartin, By Lochgilphead PA31 8RQ (05465 224). 🏵🏵 *Commended.* Situated 30 miles south of Oban, Kilmartin is a peaceful village set in an area of immense historic, archaeological and geological interest. Amenities include fishing (sea, loch and river), sailing, windsurfing, pony trekking, hill walking and bird watching. Day trips to various Western Isles can be arranged, also to castles and woodland gardens. Five miles to safe sandy beaches at Crinan Ferry. All rooms have central heating, tea/coffee making facilities and washbasins; some en-suite rooms are available. TV and log fire in residents' lounge. Home baking and cooking. Children and pets welcome. Ample parking. Garden and access to farm. Fire Certificate. Tourist Board Award. Bed and Breakfast from £13 per person, reduced rates for children. Evening Meal by arrangement.

See also Colour Display Advertisement **LOCHGAIR. Mr and Mrs Mark Reynolds, Knock Cottage, Lochgair, Lochgilphead PA31 8RZ (0546 86331).** Superbly situated in 10 acres of beautiful, wild garden, loch and field, with glorious views over Lochgair and Loch Fyne, Knock Cottage, an ancient croft with modern, comfortable additions is an ideal base for exploring mid-Argyll with its famous gardens, castles and breathtaking scenery. In Spring only one and a half hours from Glencoe ski-ing. On the route to the islands of Islay and Jura. Two bedrooms with good views are available, one double, one twin, each with private facilities. A beautiful drawing room and a characterful dining room for guests' comfort. Bed and Breakfast from £15; Dinner £14.50. SAE for brochure and booking form please.

LOCHGOILHEAD. Mrs Rosemary Dolan, The Shorehouse Inn, Lochgoilhead PA24 8AJ (03013 340). The Shorehouse Inn has seven letting rooms, central heating and double glazing. There are two family, three twin, one single and one double bedrooms. Residents' lounge, a bar of unusual character and licensed restaurant. Home cooking, bar meals. Formerly the old manse on a historic site with lochside and panoramic views looking southward down Loch Goil, situated in the village on the shore. Local amenities include water sports, fishing, pony trekking, tennis, bowls, golf, swimming pool, curling in winter and a good area for hill walking. Some rooms with private facilities. One hour travel time from Glasgow. Open all year round. Ideal for winter or summer breaks. Rates from £13.50 Bed and Breakfast.

OBAN. Mr and Mrs P. Tait, Roseneath Guest House, Dalriach Road, Oban PA34 5EQ (0631 62929). ❦❦ *Commended.* Situated in a quiet location close to the shopping centre and two minutes' walk from steamer, bus and rail terminals. Adjacent to swimming pool, bowling green, squash and tennis courts. All bedrooms (double, single, twin and family) are centrally heated and equipped with washbasins, shaver points, tea/coffee making facilities, bedside lights and electric blankets (some rooms en-suite). Excellent food. This family-run house is under the personal supervision of the resident proprietors who pride themselves on the comfort and happiness of their guests. A car is not essential but there is a private car park. Children welcome at reduced rates. Special low season rates for Senior Citizens. Send SAE for full details and brochure. AA and RAC listed.

FHG DIPLOMA WINNERS 1992

Each year we award a small number of diplomas to holiday proprietors whose services have been specially commended by our readers and the following advertisers were our FHG Diploma winners for 1992.

ENGLAND

Mr D. Spandler, Downfield Hotel, Stroud, Gloucestershire.
Mrs Margaret Jenkin, Boderloggan Farm, Wendron, Helston, Cornwall.
Mrs Jackie Cundall, Orillia House, Stockton on Forest, York.
Mrs R.J.K. Law, 38 Wheatlands Road, Paignton, Devon.
Mr and Mrs R. Jones, Sandford House Hotel, Shrewsbury, Shropshire.

SCOTLAND

Mr and Mrs J. Hamilton, Southdown Guest House, 20 Craigmillar Park, Edinburgh.
Mrs Mary McMorran, Miefield Farm, Twynholm, Kirkcudbrightshire.
Mr Henry Woodman, Cologin Homes, Lerags, by Oban, Argyll.

WALES

Mrs Margaret Cutter, Neuddlas, Tregaron, Dyfed.

OBAN. Mr and Mrs H. Davidson, "Dunmor", North Connel, Oban PA37 1RA (0631 71386).

"Dunmor" is a family run establishment offering a friendly atmosphere, comfort and good cooking. It is set in a large garden in beautiful surroundings close to the shores of Loch Etive, six miles north of Oban. Large lounge with colour TV; separate diningroom; central heating. Bedrooms have tea/coffee making facilities. Car essential, parking available. Most outdoor recreational pursuits can be enjoyed locally. Bed and breakfast from £13; Dinner (optional) £9. Open January to December. Dogs welcome.

OBAN by. Fred and Tina MacPherson, Blarcreen Farm, Bonawe, By Oban PA37 1RG (0631 75 272).

Blarcreen is a lovely Victorian farmhouse in a beautiful and secluded position on the shores of Loch Etive, 12 miles from Oban. An extensive hill sheep farm, it makes an ideal base for those interested in hill walking, fishing, bird watching and wildlife. A warm welcome, good food and comfortable accommodation awaits you on this friendly, family run farm. Six guests only at any one time. Bed and Breakfast from £13; Evening Meal £9.

PORT APPIN. Mr and Mrs R. Evans, Linnhe House, Port Appin PA38 4DE (Appin [0631 73] 245).

Linnhe House stands in unspoilt village of Port Appin amid surroundings of unsurpassed beauty and peace, with uninterrupted views across Loch Linnhe to the Morvern Hills. Walking, sailing, fishing and many other outdoor activities available locally. Mid way between Oban and Fort William on A828. Two miles from main road. Open all year round for Bed and Breakfast/Evening Meal; licensed. Fully centrally heated and double glazed; Fire Certificate. Washbasins in all bedrooms, two with showers, electric blankets, hair dryers, tea/coffee making facilities. Good homely cooking. Comfortable lounge with colour TV. Ample parking spaces. Pets not allowed in house but may be left in visitors' cars. No children under five. STB registered.

TARBERT. Mr W.G. McCheyne, Kirkland, Clachan, By Tarbert, Kintyre PA29 6XL (08804 200).
Former Manse with seven letting bedrooms. Situated by Tarbert, a fishing port and resort town on isthmus connecting Kintyre to mainland. Bed and Breakfast or Dinner, Bed and Breakfast offered; also caravan for hire with showers and toilets on site. Shops in village which is encircled by hills and overlooked by 14th century stronghold of Robert Bruce. Handy for all the islands. Further details and terms on request.

PUBLISHER'S NOTE

While every effort is made to ensure accuracy, we regret that FHG Publications cannot accept responsibility for errors, omissions or misrepresentation in our entries or any consequences thereof. Prices in particular should be checked because we go to press early. We will follow up complaints but cannot act as arbiters or agents for either party.

PLEASE ENCLOSE A STAMPED ADDRESSED ENVELOPE WITH ENQUIRIES

AYRSHIRE

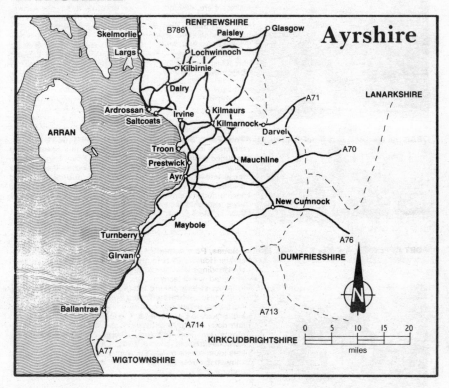

Ayrshire

AYR near. **Mrs M. Young, Garpin Farm, Crosshill, Maybole, Near Ayr KA19 7PX (Crosshill [065-54] 381 and 214). Working farm.** Comfortable, friendly accommodation is offered on this 130-acre farm, with home cooking a speciality. An excellent touring centre in very picturesque countryside, Burns country, Culzean Castle and Country Park (eight miles). Pony riding nearby. Within easy reach of lovely sandy beaches, amusements, sea fishing and golf courses, including Turnberry. One double and one twin bedrooms (both rooms are adaptable); bathroom, toilet. Lounge with open fire; diningroom. No dogs. Car essential, parking. Open March to October for Bed and Breakfast from £12 (Evening Meal optional). Mid-week bookings accepted.

BEITH. **Mrs E.W. Robertson, Burnhouse Manor, By Beith KA15 1LJ (0560 84006).** En-suite accommodation within a farmhouse setting, provides an ideal "home" for a tranquil holiday with a few added luxuries, without the added price! We are situated 50 yards from the A736 Glasgow to Irvine road, making us the perfect base for touring Burns Country, the South-West coastline, the Trossachs and Glasgow, with plenty of things to see and do for the whole family (e.g. Magnum Leisure Centre, Kelburn Country Park, Culzean Castle). Nine rooms (some family) most with en-suite and all with washbasin, colour TV, tea-making facilities and central heating. Bed and Breakfast from £12.50 per person. Personally run by the owners, the Robertson family. Brochure on request.

BEITH. Mrs Jane Gillan, Shotts Farm, Beith KA15 1LB (05055 2273). Comfortable friendly accommo-

dation is offered on this 160 acre dairy farm situated one and a half miles from the A736 Glasgow to Irvine road; well placed to visit golf courses, country parks, leisure centre or local pottery, also ideal for the ferry to Arran or Millport and many good shopping centres all around. A high standard of cleanliness is assured by Mrs Gillan who is a first class cook holding many awards, food being served in the diningroom with its beautiful picture windows. Three comfortable bedrooms (double, family and twin), all with tea-making facilities, central heating and electric blankets. Two bathrooms with shower; sittingroom with colour TV. Children welcome. Bed and Breakfast from £11; Dinner can be arranged. STB Approved.

DARVEL. Mrs J. Seton, Auchenbart Farm, Darvel, Near Priestland KA17 0LS (Darvel [0560]

20392). Working farm. Auchenbart Farmhouse is situated in an elevated position overlooking the Irvine Valley. A pleasant house offering comfortable and quiet accommodation of a high standard. One family, one twin, one double (cot available) bedrooms, all with washbasins, tea/coffee making facilities and electric blankets. Bathroom with shower. Guests' sittingroom with colour TV. Heating throughout. Access to Auchenbart is at the east end of Darvel, one mile off the A71 to Edinburgh. Darvel is famous for lace manufacturing and is the birthplace of Sir Alexander Fleming (discovered penicillin). We are central for Kilmarnock, Prestwick and Glasgow. Reductions for children. Car essential. Pets welcome. STB Listed and Commended. Open Easter till end of October. Bed and Breakfast £14 per person per night.

GIRVAN. Mrs Isobel Kyle, Hawkhill Farm, Old Dailly, Girvan KA26 9RD (0465 87232). ♥ ♥ *Highly*

Commended. **Working farm.** Superior farmhouse hospitality in spacious 16th century coaching inn where the emphasis is on comfort and good food. Two delightful bedrooms with private facilities. Visitors' lounge. Central heating, log fires. Tea trays. Peaceful setting perfect for exploring unspoilt South West Scotland. Near Culzean Castle, Galloway Forest Park, Ayr and Burns country. Golf, fishing, pony trekking. Bed and Breakfast from £16. Phone for brochure.

KILBIRNIE. Mrs E.M. Cameron, "Alpenrose", 113 Herriot Avenue, Kilbirnie KA25 7JB (0505

683122). "Alpenrose", a delightful and peaceful detached villa set amongst the hills of North Ayrshire on the outskirts of the small village of Kilbirnie, just off the A760 Largs to Kilbirnie road with the coastal town of Largs only 12 minutes' drive away. "Alpenrose" is in an excellent spot for visiting Robert Burns country, the islands of Arran, Bute and Cumbrae and the Clyde Coast. With R.S.P.B. birdwatching, hill walking, golfing and lochs with fishing and boat hire all on the doorstep it is superb for the outdoor enthusiast, or for the less energetic just relaxing in a country garden or plant-filled sun lounge which has maps, books and Scrabble all at hand. Guests call "Alpenrose" a real home from home. The lovely home cooking and fresh farm eggs, oatcakes, home made preserves served at breakfast make a good start to the day plus the very best of personal attention at all times. The bedrooms are prettily decorated; the double room has a king-size bed and all rooms have TV, tea/coffee and chocolate making facilities with supper biscuits. Light suppers or Evening Dinners are served in the very pleasant diningroom to suit guests' requirements. Do-it-yourself barbecues on patio, weather permitting. Drying facilities and showers always available. Bed and Breakfast from £9. Please send for further details and photograph of villa. Open all year.

KILMARNOCK. Mrs Mary Howie, Hill House Farm, Grassyards Road, Kilmarnock (0563 23370).

🐝🐝 *Commended.* Working dairy farm, in beautiful open countryside, offering warm welcome and home cooking. Two miles east of Kilmarnock and one mile from A77 with easy access to Ayrshire coast and Burns' country. Sport and leisure with skating, swimming pools, theatre, etc within easy reach. Three large comfortable bedrooms with wash-basins and tea/coffee making facilities; bathroom and toilet; lounge, diningroom. Central heating. Excellent walking country and ideal base for touring, enjoying golf, fishing or relaxing on sandy beaches. Bed and breakfast from £12 (including light supper). Also self catering cottage available. For further details contact **Mrs Howie.**

KILMARNOCK. Mr and Mrs A. Elliot, Old Rome Farmhouse, Gatehead, Kilmarnock KA2 9AJ (0563

850265). Old Rome is situated two miles from Kilmarnock in a completely rural setting 300 yards off the A759 to Troon. The farmhouse has charm and character; dating back to the 17th century it has recently been converted to a country inn. It offers a warm comfortable bar, log fires, extensive range of home cooked bar meals lunchtimes and evenings. Accommodation offered in four bedrooms — two double, two twin — with washbasins and tea/coffee making facilities. Bathroom adjacent to bedrooms. Lounge with colour TV. Brochure on request. Recommended, gained award in The Best of Scotland's Pubs 1991.

KILMARNOCK. Mrs M.S. Love, Muirhouse Farm, Gatehead, Kilmarnock KA2 0BT (0563 23975).
🐝🐝 *Commended.* Muirhouse is situated approximately two miles south west of Kilmarnock, adjacent to Gatehead village which is on the A759 Kilmarnock to Troon road. It is a family run 170 acre dairy/arable farm. Easy access to Ayrshire coast, Burns Country, Culzean Castle and Glasgow (Burrell Collection). Ample facilities available for all outdoor sports, plus two modern indoor sports complexes nearby. Traditional stone-built comfortable farmhouse with central heating. There is one family room (sleeping four) en-suite and one double bedroom, both with washbasins and tea-making facilities; two bathrooms; sittingroom with TV; diningroom. Children welcome, cot etc available. Car essential. Bed and Breakfast from £13 to £17. Evening Meal by arrangement. Reductions for children and also for weekly bookings. SAE, please, for terms and further details.

KNOCKENTIBER. Mr and Mrs P. Gibson, Busbiehill Guest House, Knockentiber, Near Kilmarnock KA2 0AJ (Kilmarnock [0563] 32985). This homely country guest house is situated in the heart of Burns country and is also handy for touring Loch Lomond, The Trossachs, Edinburgh and the Clyde Coast. Golf course nearby. Two single rooms; four family suites; two double rooms with bathroom; tea-making facilities. Sittingroom; two diningrooms. Children welcome; cot, high chair, swings available. Sorry, no pets. Car essential — parking space. Open from April to November. Bed and Breakfast from £10 to £14; Evening Meal £4. Fully licensed. 10 per cent discount for Senior Citizens.

LARGS. Mrs M. Watson, South Whittlieburn Farm, Brisbane Glen, Largs KA30 8SN (0475 675881).

🐝🐝 *Commended.* **Working farm.** AA listed. An attractive working sheep farm in lovely Brisbane Glen, two miles north east of Largs. Golf courses, horse riding, fishing, sailing, diving, hillwalking all available. A popular tourist centre within easy reach of Glasgow and Ayr, three-quarters of an hour from Glasgow or Prestwick Airports, near ferries for the Islands of Arran, Cumbrae and Bute. A warm welcome in comfortable accommodation with washbasins, tea/coffee facilities and colour TVs; en-suite available. TV lounge; two bathrooms. Central heating. Large private car park. Packed lunches and vegetarian meals available. Reduced rates for children under 11 years. Bed and Breakfast from £14.50. Certified caravan and camping site on farm with toilet and emptying point. From £4 per night.

NEWMILNS. Mrs Anne Mitchell, Whatriggs Farm, Newmilns KA16 9LJ (05607 279). Whatriggs is a dairy and stock rearing farm run by the family. We are ideally placed for touring central and southern Scotland as well as the West Coast. Situated one mile from A719 Galston/Glasgow road, between Galston and the village of Moscow. Children and pets welcome. One double and one family bedroom available, also single bedroom on ground floor. Bed and Breakfast from £12 to £15. Ayrshire Tourist Board registered.

Terms quoted in this publication may be subject to increase if rises in costs necessitate

CAITHNESS

LATHERON. Mrs Cath Falconer, Tacher Farm, Latheron KW5 6DX (05934 313). Working farm. A hill farm with sheep and cows. Plenty of wide open spaces to walk or bird watch. Golf and fishing can be arranged. Comfortable house with garden and parking area. Lounge with peat fire and colour TV. One bathroom with shower and separate shower room. All bedrooms have tea/coffee making facilities and the family room has washbasin. Day trips to the Orkney Islands, only 18 miles to ferry at Scrabster. Evening Meal available £8; Bed and Breakfast £12. Reduced rates for children under 12 years.

LATHERON. Mrs Camilla Sinclair, Upper Latheron Farm, Latheron KW5 6DT (05934 224). Idyllically

situated with breathtaking views of coastline and mountains. Either relax in a peaceful atmosphere or use as an excellent base for touring Northern Highlands, visiting castles, gardens, nature trails. Also ideal for visits to John O'Groats, Highland games or sheepdog trials, day trips to the Orkneys or viewing puffins and seals at Duncansby. Riding/pony trekking available at our own STRA-approved stables. New-born foals offer an additional attraction. Open May to October. Bed and Breakfast from £12; Evening Meal from £7. STB Commended. AA Approved farmhouse.

THURSO. Mrs M. Morrison, Glenearn, East Mey, Thurso KW14 8XL (084785 608). Glenearn offers

true Scottish hospitality with hearty breakfasts, tea making facilities in rooms. Sittingroom with peat fire. Central heating. Family and double rooms, ample facilities. Extra shower and toilet. One en-suite bedroom. Panoramic views of the Orkney Islands and Dunnet Head; Castle of Mey close by. Restaurant next door, Thurso 14 miles, Wick 20 miles, John O'Groats five miles where a ferry crosses daily to Orkney. Guests return year after year. French and German spoken. Bed and Breakfast from £11.50 to £12.50.

THURSO via. Mrs Nancy Geddes, Island View, East Mey, Via Thurso KW14 8XL (Barrock [084-785]

254). A warm welcome awaits guests at "Island View," a modernised cottage. Nearby is the Castle of Mey, Dunnet Head and John O' Groats, from where the ferry goes to Orkney daily. There is a panoramic view of the Orkney Isles from all bedroom windows. All beds have duck down duvets with cotton oversheets. Good food and comfort is guaranteed. One family room and one double room with washbasins and tea/coffee making facilities; guest sittingroom with TV and sun lounge; diningroom; two bathrooms and shower. Central heating throughout. Ample hot water, towels and soap supplied. Pets allowed. Bed and Breakfast from £11.50. Children and Senior Citizens at reduced terms. Ample parking. Open April to October. Tourist Board registered. SAE, please, for further details.

DUMFRIESSHIRE

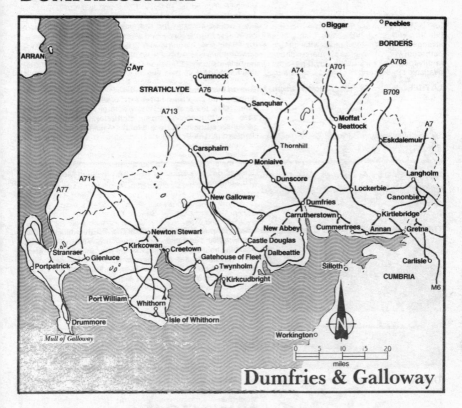

Dumfries & Galloway

BEATTOCK. Mrs Freda Bell, Cogries Farm, Beattock, Moffat DG10 9PP (05764 320). 🕊 *Commended.* **Working farm.** Cogries is a 540 acre dairy and mixed farm which lies just under half a mile off the A74 (10 miles north of Lockerbie and three miles south of Beattock). The farmhouse has four bedrooms all with washbasins and tea making facilities. Bath/shower room and separate toilet. Visitors can go salmon and sea trout fishing, train spotting, bird watching on the farm, play croquet on the lawn or just relax on the patio. An ideal stopover when travelling north or south, or as a touring base for south west Scotland. Cogries is conveniently situated for Moffat, Dumfries, Glasgow, Edinburgh, Hadrian's Wall, Carlisle and the northern Lake District. Comments from the visitors' book are very favourable and hopefully yours will be added. Bed and Breakfast from £13; Evening Meal on request. Also self catering cottage to let.

See also Colour Display Advertisement **CANONBIE. Mrs R. Clough, Brockwoodlees, Canonbie DG4 0XD (03873 71578).** Brockwoodlees is set in 1000 acres of rolling farmland surrounded by beautiful woodlands. We provide a traditional farmhouse Bed and Breakfast with many lovely walks and other sporting activities close to main A7 tourist route to Edinburgh.

DUMFRIES AND GALLOWAY REGION – BURNS' COUNTRY.
A fair sprinkling of castles, the Solway Firth coast and, of course, Burns' Country makes this region an interesting tourist destination. Other attractions include the Grey Mare's Tail, Galloway Forest Park, Caerlaverock and Clatteringshaws deer museum.

CARLISLE. Mrs G. Elwen, Newpallyards, Hethersgill, Carlisle CA6 6HZ (0228 577 308). 🦢🦢🦢

Commended. **Working farm, join in.** GOLD AWARD WINNER. Filmed for BBC TV. Relax and see North Cumbria and the Borders. A warm welcome awaits you on our 65 acre farm tucked away in the Cumbrian countryside, yet easily accessible from M6 Junction 44. In addition to the surrounding attractions there is plenty to enjoy including hill walking, peaceful forests and sea trout/salmon fishing, ponies on the farm, or just nestle down and relax with nature. Accommodation consists of two double rooms en-suite, two family rooms en-suite, one twin/single bedroom, all with tea/coffee making equipment. Bowls, putting etc for guests' enjoyment. Bed and Breakfast from £16 to £19; Dinner, Bed and Breakfast from £27.50 to £29.50. Half Board (Dinner, Bed and Breakfast) £150 to £170. Menu choice. Self-catering also available, terms on request. We are proud to have won a National Salon Culinaire Award for the Best Breakfast in Britain. AA, HWFH, FHB.

DUMFRIES. Mrs A. Burford, Allanton House, Auldgirth, Dumfries DG2 0RY (0387 74509). 🦢🦢

Allanton is attractively situated in its own grounds of 20 acres offering friendly family-run atmosphere and good food. Large gracious bedrooms, all with washbasins. We keep Belted Galloway cattle, Suffolk Cross sheep and ponies, peafowl, chickens, rabbits, etc. An ideal area for country walks and drives exploring the many woodlands and natural scenery. Good golf courses nearby, salmon fishing and pony trekking available or just relax in the peace and quiet. Terms: Bed and Breakfast double or twin room £14 per person, per night; Bed and Breakfast and Evening Meal £19 per person, per night; Bed and Breakfast single room £15 per night. Children 12 years and under half price. AA listed. Apply for full details to above address.

LOCKERBIE. Nether Boreland, Boreland, Lockerbie DG11 2LL (05766 248). Enjoy Scottish hospitality, peaceful friendly surroundings and hearty breakfasts on this 200 acre sheep and suckler cow farm in the scenic Dryfe Valley, six miles from A74. The spacious and comfortable farmhouse has two en-suite bedrooms and one with private bathroom; all have tea/coffee making facilities, hair dryers and clock radios. Separate diningroom and large sittingroom with log fires on cold evenings, and colour TV. Enjoy local golf, fishing, pony trekking or leisurely sightseeing. Farmhouse Award Winner. Bed and Breakfast from £18 to £20. Please send for brochure. Open April to November.

MOFFAT. Mrs D. Halliwell, The Old Schoolhouse, Roundstonefoot, Moffat DG10 9LG (0683 20950). Situated five miles from Moffat on the A708 Selkirk road in picturesque Moffatdale, this former village school has been transformed into a charming home in a most beautiful and peaceful setting amidst the Border hills. Accommodation consists of two double bedrooms with private bath/shower and one twin-bedded room (ground floor), all with tea/coffee making facilities. Central heating throughout. Lounge with log fire and colour TV; separate diningroom. Ample private car parking. Open April to October. Bed and Breakfast from £13 to £15 per person. STB member.

MOFFAT. Mrs Jean McKenzie, "Hidden Corner", Beattock Road, Moffat DG10 9SE (Moffat [0683] 20243). "Hidden Corner" stands in an acre of ground, only half a mile from the A74 and half a mile from Moffat. An ideal base for exploring the Borders and South West Scotland; Edinburgh, Glasgow, the east and west coasts are within one hour's drive from Moffat. In and around Moffat, which lies in the Annandale Valley, visitors can enjoy boating, putting, tennis, green bowling, fishing, golf (18-hole), hill walking and pony trekking. Accommodation comprises two double and one twin-bedded rooms, all with hot and cold water, shaver points. Central heating. Bath/shower room. Lounge with TV; diningroom. Ample parking. Open all year. Bed and Full Breakfast £12.50 to £15.

MOFFAT. Mrs Marion S. Baillie, St. Olaf Guest House, Eastgate, Moffat DG10 9AE (Moffat [0683] 20001). ✿ AA; Fire Certificate held. St. Olaf is quietly situated off the main street. It is ideally placed for overnight stops or for a relaxing holiday. A warm welcome awaits you with good food and personal attention, every effort being made to cater for individual requirements. Local facilities include golf, tennis, bowling, putting green, boating and some delightful walks. Open from April to October. Three double, one single and three family rooms all with washbasins and tea making facilities; en-suite facilities available. Bathroom, toilets and shower room; sittingroom, diningroom. Central heating installed. Children welcome, cot, high chair and babysitting offered. Car essential, free covered garaging, also street parking. Pets allowed. Bed and Breakfast. Tea and biscuits served before retiring at no extra charge. SAE, please, for further details.

Please mention this guide when you write or phone to enquire about accommodation.

If you are writing, a stamped, addressed envelope is always appreciated.

MOFFAT. Mrs Sandra Long, Coxhill Farm, Old Carlisle Road, Moffat DG10 9QN (Moffat [0683] 20471). 👑👑 *Highly Commended.* A very attractive farmhouse set in 70 acres of unspoilt countryside with outstanding views, beautiful rose gardens and ample parking. Finished inside and out to a very high standard. Accommodation comprises two double and one twin bedrooms, all with washbasins and central heating; two guests' bathrooms with shower; residents' sittingroom and diningroom. Light supper served. Bed and Breakfast from £14; Evening Meal £9. Reductions for children under 12 years. Situated one mile to the south of the charming town of Moffat, 1989 winner of the Large Village section of Scotland in Bloom. One mile from A74 and an excellent base for walking, golf, fishing, tennis, pony trekking, etc. New sports barn in Moffat.

DUNBARTONSHIRE

GLASGOW. The Patio Hotel, 1 South Avenue, Clydebank G81 2RW (041-951 1133; Fax: 041-952 3713). 👑👑👑👑 AA/RAC three stars. Not just handy for Glasgow's City Centre, this two year old hotel, has quick and easy access to the Airport, SECC, Loch Lomond, the Trossachs and the Ayrshire Coast. The hotel is built around a magnificent central atrium with fountain and towering fig tree, featuring restaurant and cocktail bar in the planted area below. All bedrooms are luxuriously furnished with en-suite bathrooms, colour TV, radio, hairdryer, trouser press, telephone and tea/coffee making facilities. Bed and Breakfast available at £30.75 per person sharing a half twin/double. Exit M8 at Junction 19 and follow signs for Clydebank.

EDINBURGH & THE LOTHIANS

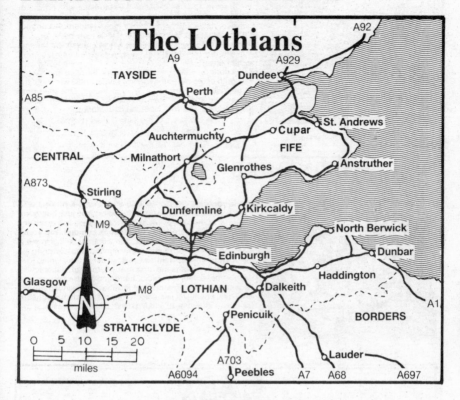

The Lothians

EDINBURGH. Mr A. Borland, Rothesay Hotel, 8 Rothesay Place, Edinburgh EH3 7SL (031-225 4125/6). Within the heart of Edinburgh's New Town, the Rothesay Hotel has 36 well-furnished bedrooms, the majority offering private bath facilities. Situated three minutes' walk from Princes Street, Edinburgh's shopping and commercial centre, the hotel provides an ideal base for exploring the charms of this historic city. The individual tourist or businessman is catered for and group bookings are also welcomed. From the Reception Foyer easy access is provided by elevator on all floors to bedrooms. Cocktail Bar and Restaurant where there is a choice of traditional Scottish cuisine and refreshments. Children are welcome at reduced rates and cot, high chair are available. Babysitting can be arranged. Suitable for the disabled guest. Pets allowed. Open all year. (High Season May/September). Reductions for Senior Citizens April, May, September and October. Prices on application.

EDINBURGH. Mrs H. Donaldson, "Invermark", 60 Polwarth Terrace, Edinburgh EH11 1NJ (031-337 1066). 🐝🐝 Invermark is a Georgian semi-detached villa situated in quiet suburbs on the main bus route into the city and only five minutes by car. Edinburgh by-pass; Lothianburn junction. Edinburgh is one of Europe's most splendid cities, famous for its dramatic beauty, historical interest, extensive shopping and dining facilities. There is a park to the rear of the house. Accommodation consists of one single, one twin and one family room (with tea-making facilities and washbasins); TV lounge/diningroom; toilet; bathroom/shower. Friendly atmosphere. Children and dogs welcome. Bed and Breakfast from £14. Reductions for children.

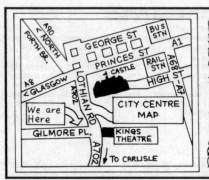

HADDINGTON. Katie Kerr, Barney Mains, Haddington EH41 3SA (062 088 310; Fax: 062 088 639).

Barney Mains Farmhouse is situated on top of a hill with wonderful panoramic views of beautiful surrounding countryside. The house is tastefully decorated and traditionally furnished, very comfortable throughout. Open fires and home baking make this a homely and pleasant place to stay. Close to many fine beaches, golf courses, pretty villages, castles and country homes. Edinburgh is only 20 minutes' drive away. Ideal for touring the Lothians and the Borders areas. Accommodation is offered in two twin rooms and one double, all with tea/coffee making facilities. STB Listed and Commended, AA Listed. Telephone or Fax for further details.

Key to
Tourist Board Ratings

The Crown Scheme
(England, Scotland & Wales)

Covering hotels, motels, private hotels, guesthouses, inns, bed & breakfast, farmhouses. Every Crown classified place to stay is inspected annually. *The classification:* Listed then 1-5 Crown indicates the range of facilities and services. Higher quality standards are indicated by the terms APPROVED, COMMENDED, HIGHLY COMMENDED and DELUXE.

The Key Scheme
(also operates in Scotland using a Crown symbol)

Covering self-catering in cottages, bungalows, flats, houseboats, houses, chalets, etc. Every Key classified holiday home is inspected annually. *The classification:* 1-5 Key indicates the range of facilities and equipment. Higher quality standards are indicated by the terms APPROVED, COMMENDED, HIGHLY COMMENDED and DELUXE.

The Q Scheme
(England, Scotland & Wales)

Covering holiday, caravan, chalet and camping parks. Every Q rated park is inspected annually for its quality standards. The more √ in the Q – up to 5 – the higher the standard of what is provided.

MUSSELBURGH. Mrs J.R.M. Dewar, "Glenesk", Delta Place, Smeaton Grove, Inveresk, Musselburgh EH21 7TP (031-665 3217). Quietly situated in the picturesque and historic village of Inveresk, "Glenesk" is a spacious detached villa convenient for all the scenic beauties, beaches and sporting activities of the east coast. Seven miles from the centre of Edinburgh and a mile from the busy shopping centre of Musselburgh. All bedrooms have private shower rooms or bathrooms, colour TV and tea-making facilities. The ground floor accommodation includes a bedroom and a comfortable lounge for guests. Bed and Breakfast from £15. Free parking. No signs displayed — conservation area. SAE please.

MUSSELBURGH. Miss A.R. Mitchell, Craigesk Guest House, 10 Albert Terrace, Musselburgh EH21 7LR (031-665 3344 or 3170). 🏵 Attractive stone-built villa overlooking racecourse and the sea, has a colourful front garden with secluded garden at rear; ample private parking. Tastefully decorated and carpeted throughout. Two double, one single and three family rooms, all with washbasins, colour TV and tea/coffee making facilities. Free electric heating. Colour TV lounge. Full Scottish breakfast. Convenient bus service to centre of Edinburgh. Guests are assured of a homely Scottish welcome all year, and will find Craigesk convenient for many sporting and entertainment facilities. Children welcome; cot and high chair provided. Suitable for the disabled. Pets allowed. Cards and Board games available. Bed and Breakfast from £13 daily. Children according to age. Fire Certificate. SAE please.

NORTH BERWICK. Mrs J. Tuer, Whitekirk Mains, Whitekirk, Dunbar (062087 245). 🏵🏵 *Highly Commended.* **Working farm.** Whitekirk Mains is a working farm with attractive period farmhouse offering 20th century comfort. Situated at the edge of a small village, it provides accommodation in large twin/family rooms, en-suite, with colour TV and tea/coffee making facilities. Sitting area with scenic views. Full central heating. Use of house throughout the day. East Lothian offers safe, sandy, beaches, beautiful countryside, quiet roads, historic houses and superb restaurants. Ideal area for fishing, walking and golf — 12 courses are within 12 miles of Whitekirk. Close to sea; 30 minutes from Edinburgh. SAE please for terms or telephone.

PATHHEAD. Mrs Margaret Winthrop, "Fairshiels", Blackshiels, Pathhead EH7 5SX (087-533 665). Situated on the A68, 15 miles south of Edinburgh and about 10 miles from the coast, on the bus route to Edinburgh. The house was once a coaching inn. All rooms are spacious and comfortably furnished. There is a colour TV in the lounge, separate diningroom. We have one double and five family bedrooms for guests, all with washbasins. Children are welcome and there is a cot, a high chair and babysitting is offered. Open all year round with central heating and fires. Pets allowed. Car is not essential, but there is parking. Bed and Breakfast from £11.50 per night which includes a bedtime drink; £6.50 per child, under two years free.

FIFE

AUCHTERMUCHTY. Mrs I.J. Steven, Ardchoille Farmhouse, Woodmill, Auchtermuchty (Tel and Fax: 0337 28414). 🌼🌼🌼 *Highly Commended.* Welcome

to Ardchoille, a spacious well appointed farmhouse where guests are assured of every comfort and a high standard of food. Excellent home cooking, delicious breakfasts including home made preserves; dinners include home made soups, pates, roasts, trout and salmon, home grown vegetables. "Taste of Scotland" recommended. Farmhouse sleeps six. All rooms en-suite (two twin, one twin/family) with colour TV and tea-making (home made shortbread provided). Ideal base for touring Scotland and for golfing, Edinburgh one hour, St. Andrews 20 minutes. Bed and Breakfast from £22. FHB Member. Two fully equipped five-berth caravans for hire. Pony riding on site. Also available, self catering holiday house. SAE for brochure.

SCOTTISH FARMHOUSE HOLIDAYS. 🌼🌼🌼 *Highly Commended.* Dinner, Bed and Breakfast from £17

Scottish Farmhouse Holidays

per person per night or Bed and Breakfast from £13 per person per night in over 80 personally inspected farm and croft houses. You can choose to stay at any farm or tour around our beautiful country, staying a few nights at different farmhouses, where the warm welcome and home baking will ensure a holiday to remember. Also a few self catering properties. The central reservation system makes planning these holidays easy, so get your free brochure now. Contact: **Jane Buchanan, 7 Drumtenant, Ladybank, Fife KY7 7UG (0337 30451/830451 24 hour answering service or Fax 0337 31301/831301 from February 1993).**

ST. ANDREWS. Mrs Anne Duncan, Spinkstown Farmhouse, St. Andrews KY16 8PN (0334 73475).

Working farm. Only two miles from St. Andrews on the picturesque A917 coast road to Crail, Spinkstown is a uniquely designed farmhouse with views of the sea and surrounding countryside. Bright and spacious, it is furnished to a high standard. Accommodation consists of double and twin rooms, all with wash hand basins or en-suite facilities; dining room and lounge with colour TV. Substantial farmhouse breakfast to set you up for the day; evening meals are by arrangement only. The famous Old Course, historic St. Andrews and several National Trust properties are all within easy reach as well as swimming, tennis, putting, bowls, horse riding, country parks, nature reserves, beaches and coastal walks. Plenty of parking available. Bed and Breakfast from £14 to £17; Evening Meal £10. AA listed.

INVERNESS-SHIRE

[Map of Inverness-shire region showing locations including Gairloch, Staffin, Uig, Culnacnock, Achnasheen, Dingwall, Nairn, A9, A96, Dunvegan, Portree, Struan, RAASAY, Applecross, ROSS-SHIRE, Beauly, Culloden, Croy, Ardersier, Kirkhill, Inverness, Daviot, A939, Strome Ferry, SCALPAY, Kyle of Lochalsh, Milton, Drumnadrochit, Moy, Tomatin, Grantown, SKYE, Broadford, Breakish, Invermoriston, Foyers, Carrbridge, Dulnain Br, Boat of Garten, Nethy-bridge, Clunie, Fort Augustus, Loch Ness, Aviemore, Teangue, CANNA, Invergarry, Newtonmore, Kingussie, Kincraig, RHUM, EIGG, Arisaig, MUCK, Spean Bridge, Roy Bridge, Corpach, Fort William, A93, PERTHSHIRE, Onich, ARGYLL, A828, and a scale bar in miles. Labelled "Inverness-shire"]

BEAULY. Mrs M.M. Ritchie, Rheindown Farm, Beauly IV4 7AB (Beauly [0463] 782461). 👑👑 *Commended.* **Working farm, join in.** Fifty acres with magnificent views overlooking Beauly Valley and Firth, across to Inverness, Black Isle and round to Ben Wyvis. Beef cattle and sheep are kept on farm. For the children there are free range hens to be fed and ducks, usually pet lambs to feed by bottle and they can watch the House Cow being milked by hand. One family room and one double bedroom available, both with washbasins and tea/coffee making facilities; bathroom downstairs; diningroom and sittingroom for guests. Children welcome, cot, babysitting by arrangement. Pets allowed. Open April to October with solid fuel/oil central heating. Excellent centre for day trips to North and West coasts, bus tours, cruises down Loch Ness; golf, fishing, pony trekking, boating, all locally. Pleasant walks nearby and hill climbing for the adventurous. Dinner, Bed and Breakfast from £18.50; Bed and Breakfast from £13.50. Reduced rates for children under 15 years.

CARRBRIDGE. Mr and Mrs M. Stitt, Carrmoor Guest House, Carr Road, Carrbridge PH23 3AD (Carrbridge [047-984] 244). 👑👑 *Commended.* Family-run, AA listed QQQ, Licensed Guest House in beautiful Highland village of Carrbridge. Excellent base for pony trekking, hill walking, golf, fishing, sailing, ski-ing and bird watching: RSPB Bird Sanctuary within easy reach. Evening entertainment locally and at Aviemore. Open all year round. Cosy guest lounge with open log fire. All bedrooms have central heating, electric blankets, tea/coffee facilities. En-suite rooms available. Child reductions. Pets welcome. Available to guests: baby listening, iron, hairdryer. Packed lunches. Special diets by arrangement. Good drying room/ski store. Bed and Breakfast from £13.50 per night low season, £14.50 high season; Dinner, Bed and Breakfast from £23.00 low season, £24.00 high season. Weekly rates on request.

CARRMOOR GUEST HOUSE

CARRBRIDGE. Mrs Lynn Benge, The Pines Guest House, Duthill, Carrbridge PH23 3ND (047-984

220). Relax and enjoy the excellent facilities of this country guesthouse situated in the peaceful surroundings of a pine forest, just two miles from Carrbridge. This is an ideal base for touring, golf, pony trekking, bird watching, fishing, hill walking, ski-ing, water sports, 4x4 outdoor adventures. The guesthouse offers comfortable accommodation in one family, one double and one twin bedrooms, all with washbasins; separate lounge with TV. Tea/coffee facilities. Oil-fired central heating. Cot, high chair and babysitting available. A car is essential, parking available. Traditional and vegetarian cooking. Pets welcome by arrangement. Dinner, Bed and Breakfast or Bed and Breakfast only. Bed and Breakfast from £13 to £14. Please send SAE for terms and further details. STB Listed and Commended.

CARRBRIDGE. Roger and Liz Reed, Fairwinds Hotel, Carrbridge PH23 3AA (047984 240). 👑👑👑

Highly Commended. AA Selected, RAC Highly Acclaimed. Experience a true Highland welcome. Dine on Scotland's finest produce — Speyside Trout, Salmon, Venison, cheeses and many others. Relax in pleasant comfortable surroundings in front of a real fire. Perhaps glimpse a shy Roe deer from your bedroom. All our rooms are en-suite and centrally heated. Our guests are assured of personal attention at all times. Vegetarian meals and packed lunches are available by arrangement. Sorry, no dogs. Many activities locally, or just have a rest. Allow us to make your holiday memorable. Please write or phone for further details.

CULLODEN MOOR. Mrs E.M.C. Alexander, Culdoich Farm, Culloden Moor IV1 2EP (Inverness [0463] 790268). 👑👑 *Commended.* **Working farm.** A true Highland welcome awaits you at Culdoich Farm, a 140-acre mixed farm. This is a well-furnished Inverness-shire farmhouse, situated in the valley of the River Nairn, seven miles from Inverness and two miles from the famous Culloden Moor. Nairn's beach only 10 miles away and Aviemore Sports Centre, Loch Ness, Cawdor Castle etc, are all worth visits. Good farmhouse food. Lots of home baking. One double, one family room, both with washbasins and tea/coffee making facilities; bathroom, toilet; sittingroom, diningroom. Children welcome with cot, high chair, babysitting offered. Car essential — parking. No pets. Opes Easter to October. Evening Dinner, Bed and Breakfast or Bed and Breakfast. Reductions for children. Farm Holiday Guide Diploma winner. SAE brings prompt reply.

See also Colour Display Advertisement **DAVIOT. Torguish House, Daviot (0463 772208).** 👑👑👑

Commended. The world famous author of "HMS Ulysses" and "The Guns of Navarone" and 17 other major novels which enthral millions, spent his formative childhood years in Torguish House. Once the local manse it is now an extremely homely guesthouse offering nine bedrooms, four having en-suite facilities. Welcoming log fire with big accommodating armchairs are in the TV lounge. Torguish House enjoys having children stay and provides a special adventure play area. The location is ideal for touring and golf and fishing are available nearby. Bed and Breakfast from £11; Dinner, Bed and Breakfast from £18; en-suite Bed and Breakfast from £15, en-suite Dinner, Bed and Breakfast from £22. Child under two years free; two to eight years Bed and Breakfast from £7; over eight years en-suite £11. A fully detailed brochure is available on request.

DULNAIN BRIDGE. Mr and Mrs A. Watson, Rosegrove Guest House, Skye of Curr, Dulnain Bridge, Grantown-on-Spey PH26 3PA (047-985 335). 👑👑

Commended. Situated close to the famous heather centre, in the beautiful Spey Valley, 10 miles from Aviemore. Ideal for birdwatching, walking, fishing or golf and exploring the mountains and glens of the Scottish Highlands. The food here is something special, venison, salmon and Scotch beef (bring your own wine). After dinner relax by the log fire enjoying the view over the valley to the Cairngorms. Accommodation is in double, twin, single and family rooms, some en-suite. On arrival guests are served with tea and home baking. Large car park. Pets welcome. Open at Christmas and New Year. Dinner, Bed and Breakfast from £20; Bed and Breakfast from £13.50. Weekly terms available.

FORT WILLIAM. J. and E. Rosie, Guisachan Guest House, Alma Road, Fort William (0397 703797). Delightfully situated in own grounds overlooking Loch Linnhe and Ardgour Hills, yet within five minutes walking of bus and railway stations and town centre. Well placed for day trips to Inverness, Isle of Skye, Oban, Inveraray, Pitlochry, etc.; for the more energetic there is excellent walking, climbing and fishing, and ski-ing in the winter and early spring. We offer good home cooking and a variety of wines and also a fine selection of malt whiskies to choose from. Rooms have en-suite with tea/coffee facilities and colour TV. A warm welcome awaits you. Open January to November. Bed and Breakfast from £18 to £24.

See also Colour Display Advertisement **FORT WILLIAM. Mrs L. MacGregor, Achnabobane Farmhouse, By Spean Bridge, Fort William (Spean Bridge [039-781] 342). Working farm.** On main A82 road, this 100-acre hill farm with herd of Highland cattle has south-facing farmhouse overlooking Ben Nevis. Ideally situated for hill walking, fishing, shooting or touring. Comfortable bedrooms with washbasins and kettles for evening 'cuppas'. Children welcome. Bed and Breakfast from £13; Evening Dinner, Bed and Breakfast from £21. Open all year round and Highly Recommended.

FORT WILLIAM. Glenlochy Guest House, Nevis Bridge, Fort William PH33 6PF (0397 702909). ❤❤ *Commended.* AA listed. Fully modernised guest house situated in own spacious grounds close to main A82 road. Halfway between Ben Nevis and Town Centre and at official end of West Highland Way Walk. 10 rooms, eight with private facilities, all with colour TV, tea/coffee making facilities. Warmth and cleanliness guaranteed. Access to rooms at all times. Payphone. Private car park. SAE for colour brochure and tariff.

FORT WILLIAM. Mrs M. Matheson, Thistle Cottage, Torlundy, Fort William (0397 702428). Thistle

Cottage is in a rural area, two miles from Nevis Range Ski Centre, set in beautiful quiet valley below Aonach Mor and Ben Nevis. It is three and a half miles from Fort William town centre; central for touring the Highlands. Warm and friendly welcome with tea/coffee served in lounge. Two bedrooms — one double and one family, one with private bathroom. Bed and Breakfast from £12.50 per person per night. Reduction for children. Large parking area. Pets welcome.

FORT WILLIAM near. Mr and Mrs A.G. Ward, Glen Loy Lodge, Banavie, Near Fort William PH33 7PD

(Spean Bridge [039-781] 700). ❤❤❤ *Commended.* Glen Loy Lodge is a well-appointed, comfortable country house providing good food and wine, in a warm, friendly, relaxed atmosphere. Situated in its own grounds by the River Loy amid deer forest, river, loch and mountain. Close to Fort William and Ben Nevis. Ideal base for walking, climbing, fishing and motoring. Centrally heated. Seven double, two single bedrooms, some with private facilities, all with wash-basins; two bathrooms, three toilets; two sittingrooms, diningroom. Children welcome, cot available. Car essential, ample parking. Residential licence. Open all year. Evening Dinner, Bed and Breakfast or Bed and Breakfast. Rates on application, reduced for children. The Lodge has a boat on Loch Arkaig, fishing free to guests.

See also Colour Display Advertisement **FORT WILLIAM. Mr and Mrs A. Dewar, Cuilcheanna House, Onich, Fort William PH33 6SD (Onich [085-53] 226).** Cuilcheanna House is peacefully situated in its own grounds just off the main A82 road in the village of Onich. We offer our guests a combination of modern amenities and old-fashioned hospitality. All our bedrooms have en-suite facilities and tea-making equipment. Our diningroom has wonderful views down Loch Linnhe, and food is traditionally prepared using fresh produce. Licensed. Dinner, Bed and Breakfast. Please write for brochure.

FORT WILLIAM near. Mrs F.A. Nisbet, Dailanna Guest House, Kinlocheil, Near Fort William PH33 7NP (Kinlocheil [039-783] 253). 🏵🏵 *Commended.*

Dailanna is a small family run guest house situated in an elevated position overlooking Locheil on the grounds of Altdarroch Farm. It is 10 miles west of Fort William on the road to the Isles and is ideally situated as a base for touring Lochaber and the surrounding area. Good food a speciality — farm cream and eggs, roast beef, lamb, chicken, pork and salmon and trout when available. All bedrooms have washbasins, electric blankets, shaver points and tea/coffee making facilities. Guests have use of two lounges, one non-smoking, both with colour TV and picture window looking onto Locheil. Diningroom with separate tables. Two bathrooms, both with separate shower unit. Car park. Guests return year after year. Dinner, Bed and Breakfast from £22.50 to £25; Bed and Breakfast from £15 to £17.50. Weekly Dinner, Bed and Breakfast from £145 to £160. SAE, please.

INVERGARRY. Mrs Frances Jamieson, Lilac Cottage, South Laggan, Spean Bridge PH34 4EA (08093 410). Country cottage situated on the A82 in the heart of the Great Glen. Ideal for touring, walking, hill climbing, birdwatching, fishing and, in the winter, ski-ing. Aonach Mor 18 miles, Inverness 50, Fort William 23, Spean Bridge 14, Invergarry two. Accommodation comprises one double, one twin and one family bedrooms, all with washbasins. Residents' lounge with colour TV. Centrally heated and double glazed. Open all year. Write or telephone for terms and full details.

INVERGARRY. Mrs Margaret Waugh, North Laggan Farmhouse, Invergarry, By Spean Bridge PH34 4EB (080-93 335).

Two miles south of Invergarry and half a mile off the A82, North Laggan Farmhouse, once a family croft, has been fully modernised by owners Bill and Maggie Waugh, yet retains many traditional features. Overlooking the Great Glen, Loch Oich and high forested mountains, it is ideal for touring Skye, Fort William, Loch Ness and Aviemore. Hill walking available. Accommodation in one family room and one twin room, both with washbasins, tea-making facilities and TV. Good home cooking including home-made bread. Scottish Tourist Board listed and Commended. Bed and Breakfast £13.50; Dinner, Bed and Breakfast £22. Reductions for children and weekly bookings. Open May to September. Also self catering flat £100 to £290 per week.

INVERGARRY. Mrs H. Fraser, "Ardfriseal", Mandally, Invergarry PH35 4HR (Invergarry [08093] 281). Working farm. "Ardfriseal" is a modern bungalow two miles south-west of the village of Invergarry one mile off A82 with outlook on river. Central for touring, hill walking, bird watching, etc. Fishing and pony trekking available in the area. Modern bungalow accommodation. All bedrooms have washbasins. Tea/coffee making facilities. Central heating. Log fires. Skye ferry one and a quarter hours' drive. Open May to October. Dinner, Bed and Breakfast from £20.00; Bed and Breakfast only from £12.00.

See also Colour Display Advertisement   INVERGARRY. Mr and Mrs Roy Wilson, Ardgarry Farm, Faichem, Invergarry PH35 4HS (Invergarry [080 93] 226). 🏵🏵 Working farm. Try relaxing on a small working farm in a traditional Scottish farmhouse and lodge. (Plenty of animals and a children's pony). Good home cooking, cosy bedrooms, comfortable lounge/diningroom with panoramic views across the Glen to Ben Tee (2,950 ft). Ideally situated for exploring the Highland Region, whether by car or on foot. Good fishing, beautiful forest walks. Visit Loch Ness, Skye, Aviemore and the lovely Glen Garry. Substantial Dinner, Bed and Breakfast £17.50 per person per day; Bed and Breakfast from £12. All rooms have washbasins, tea/coffee making facilities. Central heating. Ample parking. Self catering also available.

INVERGARRY. Mrs Joan O'Connell, Faichem Lodge, Faichem, Invergarry PH35 4HG (Invergarry [080-93] 314). Quietly situated within a mixed farm, Faichem Lodge has been tastefully renovated, retaining its olde worlde charm, but with all modern amenities. Surrounded by mountains yet within easy reach of Fort William and Inverness. The comfortable bedrooms have washbasins, tea-making facilities and a lovely view across the Glen. Central heating throughout. We have a large oak-beamed lounge/diningroom (colour TV) and additional sun lounge. Bed and Breakfast from £13.50. Pets welcome. AA listed.

See also Colour Display Advertisement **INVERNESS. Ardmuir House, 16 Ness Bank, Inverness IV2 4SF (0463 231151).** ⚘⚘⚘ *Commended*. Situated beside the River Ness this family run Hotel, close to the town centre and Ness Islands, offers the ideal base for touring the Highlands. All bedrooms have en-suite facilities, hair dryer, colour TV and tea making. Our non-smoking diningroom, with benefit of a residents' licence, offers home cooking with fresh local produce. Dinner, Bed and Breakfast from £32 per day. Brochure and tariff available with discounts for stays of three days or more.

INVERNESS by. Mrs P. Alexander, Balaggan Farm, Culloden Moor, By Inverness IV1 2EL (0463 790213). This comfortable farmhouse set in quiet, peaceful countryside, close to Clava Cairns and standing stones, central for touring Highlands. One family and one twin bedrooms. Relax in front of open peat fire in sittingroom with colour TV. Sample the warm hospitality and the good home cooking offered at this small stock rearing farm of 90 acres. Children welcome, cot and high chair available. Dogs by arrangement. Bed and Breakfast from £13; Evening Dinner (optional) £8.

KINCRAIG, Aviemore 5 miles. Mrs S.A. Paisley, Kirkbeag, Kincraig, Kingussie PH21 1ND (0540 651298). We welcome travellers to share our unusual family home, a converted 19th century church. Centrally situated in beautiful Strathspey, an ideal location for leisurely touring. Locally arranged outdoor activities include walking, sailing, fishing, bird watching, pony trekking, golf and ski-ing or join one our our own courses in silversmithing, lapidary, wood carving or turning, ideally suited to the beginner. One twin, one double/family room. Guest TV lounge. Regret no pets. Bed and Breakfast from £13.50 per night. Dinner by arrangement. Reductions for children. Open all year. Scottish Tourist Board Listed and Commended.

KINCRAIG. Mr and Mrs E. Hayes, March House, Feshiebridge, Kincraig PH21 1NG (0540 651388). ⚘ *Commended*. This very comfortable guest house is situated in beautiful, unspoilt Glenfeshie. Perfect for all outdoor pursuits including golf and water sports (six golf courses within easy reach) and an absolute joy for the naturalist. All of the rooms have private bathroom or shower and March House has a reputation for interesting freshly prepared meals. Reduced prices for children under 14. AA listed. Taste of Scotland recommended. Dinner, Bed and Breakfast from £26. Good weekly rates. "Ideal base for a happy holiday".

KINGUSSIE. Mrs J. Stewart, Inverton House, Kingussie PH2 1NR (Kingussie [0540] 661866). Inverton House is in a secluded setting with access from the A9 on the outskirts of Kingussie, an excellent stop-over for people travelling north or south. This is an area full of historic interest, and with recreational facilities including golf, fishing, pony trekking, sailing, and Sports Centre at Aviemore all within easy reach. A warm welcome, good food with generous portions, and every comfort is offered to guests all year. Accommodation comprises one family, one double and one single bedrooms, bathroom with shower, two toilets. Heating throughout. Bed and Breakfast from £11.50 with coffee and tea available at no extra cost. Evening Dinner optional. Reductions for children. Parking space.

KINGUSSIE. John and Lorraine Walsh, Avondale, Newtonmore Road, Kingussie PH21 1HF (0540 661731). Avondale was built by the Count of Serra Largo in 1907 and offers comfortable accommodation in two family, two twin and two double rooms (two with private facilities). One guests' bathroom with toilet, one shower room with toilet, and one separate toilet. Kingussie, the capital of Badenoch, is centrally located for touring the whole of Scotland. The Whisky Trail, forest walks, mountain climbing, golf, fishing, shooting, pony trekking, tennis, falconry, gliding are just a few of the things to entertain you on your holiday. Kingussie lies about ten miles south of Aviemore, and is a stop on the mainline rail link between London and Inverness. Bed and Breakfast £15 to £18, Dinner £7.50. No smoking throughout. STB Listed "Commended".

NEWTONMORE. Kathy and Bill Sharp, Spey Valley Lodge, Station Road, Newtonmore PH20 1AR (0540 673398). Situated in half an acre of secluded grounds in a beautiful area with magnificent views. Personally supervised by owners to ensure the comfort of a Scottish welcome; traditional cooking. Numerous pursuits available — pony trekking, tennis, sailing, golf etc — in an area convenient for the Cairngorms and other mountains. Lochs and castles to visit, ski-ing available in winter. Six bedrooms (two single, one twin and three family), all with washbasins, central heating, colour TV and tea/coffee making facilities. Two shower rooms. Children's rates by request. Evening Meal on request. Pets welcome. Terms from £14.00. Mountain bikes available for hire. STB registered.

ONICH (Fort William). Mrs J. MacLean, Foresters Bungalow, Inchree, Onich, Fort William PH33 6SE (Onich [085-53] 285). Situated a quarter mile from A82 adjacent to Glen Righ Forest in quiet and peaceful surroundings. Centrally situated for touring the North West Highlands. Forest walks and trails close by and hill climbing within easy reach. Enjoy good home cooking in a friendly atmosphere. One family and two twin-bedded rooms with washbasins; bathroom, toilet and shower facilities. Colour TV lounge, diningroom. Central heating throughout. Children welcome. Dogs allowed. Car parking. Open April to October. Dinner, Bed and Breakfast from £18; Bed and Breakfast from £12 daily per person. Children's rates according to age. Reductions for weekly bookings.

ONICH (Fort William). Mrs K.A. MacCallum, Tigh-a-Righ House, Onich, Fort William PH33 6SE (08553 255). *Commended.*

Tigh-a-Righ is run on small hotel lines with a very friendly homely atmosphere where a warm Highland welcome awaits you. This family run guest house offers every comfort and good fresh food with a well stocked bar and wine list. An ideal touring base for the scenic West Highlands, close by the Corran car ferry (Loch Linnhe) and on easy routes to Glencoe and the Great Glen. By a fishing river and a short half mile walk to Loch Linnhe. Bright and well-equipped bedrooms — three double with private facilities, three family, all with washbasins, central heating, radios and tea-making; bathroom, separate shower room, two toilets. Large split level lounge, colour TV; dining-room. Centrally heated and suitable for disabled guests. Excellent meals specially prepared by expert staff. Morning teas, snack lunches and afternoon tea on request. Bed, Breakfast and Dinner from £22; en-suites £25 with reductions for children and Senior Citizens (out of season). Pets welcome. Cot and babysitting available. Parking space — a car is advantageous. Open January to December, excellent base for a ski-ing holiday. Fire Certificate. AA QQ, and RAC listed. Phone or SAE please.

SPEAN BRIDGE. Mrs M.H. Cairns, Invergloy House, Spean Bridge PH34 4DY (Spean Bridge [039-781] 681; from Summer 1993 [0397] 712681).

Commended. Converted coach house and stables furnished in tasteful comfort, in 50-acre secluded woodland grounds, overlooking Loch Lochy in Great Glen. Three twin-bedded rooms; two bathrooms with showers. Guests' sittingroom has superb view over loch and mountains. Central heating. Youngsters over eight years welcome. Free fishing (trout) from private beach reached by footpath. Rowing boats and rods for hire. Hard tennis court, rackets for hire. Ideal place for peaceful holiday, exploring Highlands, Loch Ness, Skye, Oban, Cairngorms and lovely forest and hill walks. Golf, pony trekking nearby. Open all year, long or short stays. Bed and Breakfast from £15; Evening Meal from £8. "Non-smoking" house. Tourist Board registered. SAE, please, for further details.

SPEAN BRIDGE (near Fort William). Niall and Sukie Scott, Old Pines, Gairlochy Road, Spean Bridge PH34 4EG (039-781 324; Fax: 039-781 433; from Summer 1993, 0397 712324; Fax: 0397 712433).

Commended. Old Pines is a happy family home on a smallholding quietly situated in 30 acres next to the famous Commando Memorial, sharing the same breathtaking views of Aonoch Mor (ski-ing four miles) and Ben Nevis. You are assured of a friendly welcome from Niall, Sukie and their family. Guests enjoy the relaxing, informal atmosphere, pretty en suite bedrooms, books and log fires — but especially the food! Imaginative fresh local produce carefully prepared and presented ensures memorable daily meals, served in our new conservatory. We are not licensed — bring your own wine. Children under 10 years free accommodation. Open all year. Good weekly rates. Access for completely disabled. No Smoking indoors. Taste of Scotland Member. Old Pines really is "a very special place."

TOMATIN. Glenan Lodge Licensed Guest House, Tomatin, Inverness IV13 7YT (08082 217).

Mike and Anita Moore welcome you to their relaxed and friendly guest house. Open fires, home cooking, washbasins and tea making facilities. Shower and bathrooms. Sitting room with TV, diningroom with bar. Hills and pine woods, ideal for touring, walking, bird watching, golfing or just relaxing and doing nothing. Tomatin is 15 miles south of Inverness; many places of interest are close by including Osprey Sanctuary, Loch Ness, Culloden, Moray Firth, Cawdor Castle, Fort George. The Lodge has two miles of trout/salmon fishing on the River Findhorn. Our home is your home, we personally make sure you enjoy your stay with us. Bed and Breakfast £14; Dinner £7.

KIRKCUDBRIGHTSHIRE

CASTLE DOUGLAS. Mrs Pauline Smith, Bread and Beer Cottage, Corsock, Castle Douglas DG7 3QL (064-44 652). Peace and quiet amidst attractive and friendly surroundings at "Bread and Beer Cottage", originally an 18th century drovers' inn situated in spectacular upland scenery, with easy access to A712. Dumfries 18 miles and the market town of Castle Douglas 13 miles. Fishing in Lowes Farm stream or nearby New Galloway. One double and one family room; bathroom, toilet. Central heating; electric blankets and electric heaters. Colour TV. Children welcome but sorry, no pets. Ample parking. Good plain food and home baking. Open March till November for Bed and Breakfast from £11; Evening Meal £5.

CASTLE DOUGLAS. Mrs F. Cannon, Collin Hill, Auchencairn, Castle Douglas DG7 1QN (055-664 242). ❦ ❦ *Highly Commended.* Spend a relaxing holiday at

Collin Hill Farmhouse, tastefully furnished with every comfort and spectacular views over the Solway Firth to Cumbrian Hills. Sea and village within walking distance and many leisure activities, golf courses, etc are easily reached. Galloway is renowned for its historical interest and there are also many places of scenic beauty, gardens, etc to visit. Quiet roads make touring in the area a pleasure. Two rooms en-suite, tea/coffee facilities and hairdryers. Lounge with TV. Central heating in all rooms. Vegetarians catered for. Open February to November. Bed and Breakfast £17 per person. SAE for further details please.

CROSSMICHAEL (Galloway). Mr James C. Grayson, Culgruff House Hotel, Crossmichael DG7 3BB (Crossmichael [055-667] 230). Culgruff is a former

Baronial Mansion standing in its own grounds of over 35 acres, overlooking the beautiful Ken Valley and the loch beyond. The hotel is comfortable, ideal for those seeking a quiet, restful holiday. An excellent position for touring Galloway and Burns country. The hotel is half a mile from A713 Castle Douglas to Ayr road, four miles from Castle Douglas and A75 to Stranraer. Many places of interest in the region — picturesque Solway coast villages, gardens, castles (including Culzean), the Ayrshire coast. For holiday activities — tennis, riding, pony trekking, bowls, golf, fishing (salmon, fly, coarse and sea), boating, water ski-ing, windsurfing, swimming etc. Lovely walks. All rooms have washbasins (some en-suite), electric blankets; ample bathroom/toilet facilities. All bedrooms have TVs. Large family room available. One of the lounges has colour TV; diningroom. Central heating. Children under 10 years at reduced rates. Cot. Car advisable, parking. Bed and Breakfast from £16 (including VAT); all meals available. Open from Easter to October. Restricted October to Easter. AA** and RAC**. Tourist Board registered. Home of author James Crawford.

TWYNHOLM. Mrs Mary McMorran, Miefield Farm, Twynholm, Kirkcudbright DG6 4PS (Twynholm [05576] 254). Miefield is a modern farmhouse with all modern conveniences. It is situated in 1700 acres of heather-clad hills where black-faced sheep and Galloway cattle are farmed and collie dogs can be seen at work. Ideal for walks and birdwatching, golf courses and safe sandy beaches six to nine miles away. Children most welcome to help with the feeding of pet lambs, calves etc. All home cooking and home baking at Miefield. Diningroom, sittingroom, two family rooms, double room. Open Easter — October. Car essential. Bed, Breakfast and Evening Dinner or Bed and Breakfast only. SAE for terms, or phone.

LANARKSHIRE

ABINGTON. Mrs Hodge, Gilkerscleugh Farm, Abington ML12 6SQ (08642 388). Farm accommodation in one double and one twin-bedded rooms; residents' lounge and TV for guests' use. Situated two miles off A74 and surrounded by scenic views. Children welcome with reduced rates, cot, babysitting/listening service and play area. The establishment is heated throughout. Indoor clothes drying and ironing facilities. Parking. Open May to October. Bed and Breakfast from £12 per person; Bed, Breakfast and Evening Meal from £17.

BIGGAR. Mrs A. Barrie, Howburn Farm, Elsrickle, By Biggar ML12 6JZ (089981 276). Howburn Farm is situated in the village of Elsrickle amid beautiful country surroundings. Golf and fishing within easy reach and the market town of Biggar is three and a half miles away. Good touring area, convenient for the Borders as well as Edinburgh and Glasgow. Accommodation in one twin and one family bedroom with tea-making facilities. Residents' lounge with TV; bathroom, shower. Children are welcome at reduced rates, cot and babysitting available. Garden with play area; parking. Open April to October. Bed and Breakfast from £11 to £14 per person. Full Board available. Details on request.

GLASGOW. Carole and Ewing Divers, Kirkland House, 42 St. Vincent Crescent, Glasgow G3 8NG

(041-248 3458). City Centre guesthouse offering excellent rooms, private facilities, central heating, colour TV, tea/coffee makers. Situated in a beautiful early Victorian crescent facing onto the Scottish Exhibition Centre. Also within walking distance of the museum and art gallery. Convenient for all first class restaurants and city centre facilities. Singles £30/£35. Twins/doubles £50/£55.

GLASGOW. Mr Robert Scott, Scott's Guest House, 417 North Woodside Road, Glasgow G20 6NN (041-339 3750). We are one mile from the city centre on the banks of the River Kelvin, in a quiet cul-de-sac terrace. We are within walking distance of Glasgow University, Kelvingrove Park, Art Gallery and Transport Museum, just 40 metres from Kelvinbridge tube station. Accommodation comprises double, twin, single and family rooms, all with colour TV and tea/coffee making facilities. A warm welcome awaits you at Scott's Guest House. Plenty of parking available. Open all year round. Bed and Breakfast from £15.

LANARK. Mrs J. Lamb, Hillhouse Farm, Sandilands, Lanark ML11 9TX (Douglas Water [055588]

661). Working farm. This traditional 17th century farmhouse is situated six miles from the market town of Lanark. It is one hour from both Glasgow and Edinburgh and a similar distance from the Ayrshire Coast and Burns Country. Beef and sheep farm with a stud of Clydesdale Horses. Full central heating. Accommodation comprises one double and one twin bedrooms; lounge with TV accessible at all times. Tea served with plenty of home baking. Open all year round. Bed and Breakfast from £12; Bed, Breakfast and Evening Meal from £17. A warm welcome to all visitors.

MORAYSHIRE

GRANTOWN-ON-SPEY. David and Katherine Elder, Kinross House, Woodside Avenue, Grantown-

on-Spey PH26 3JR (0479 2042). ♛♛♛ *Commended.* Peacefully situated Victorian villa in delightful country town. The warm, restful and spacious bedrooms (four en suite and one on ground floor) all have tea/coffee making trays and TV. Delicious traditional dinner is served by David in his MacIntosh kilt (sorry, no dinner Wednesdays). Table licence. Children over seven years welcome. No smoking house. Bed and Breakfast from £16 to £22. Special Spring and Autumn Breaks. True Highland hospitality from your Scottish hosts, David and Katherine Elder. Send for brochure.

PERTHSHIRE

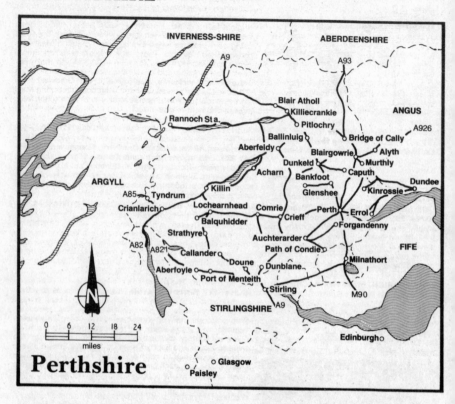

Perthshire

BALLINLUIG. Mr and Mrs R.L. Campbell, Pitnacree Cottage Guest House, Ballinluig, Pitlochry PH9 0LW (0887 840271). Beautifully situated in its own gardens overlooking the River Tay, this charming stone-built guest house has four double, two single and two family rooms, all with washbasins; two bathrooms, three toilets and shower. Bedrooms are very well appointed and have tea-making facilities. Spacious lounge with TV, accessible to guests at all times. Unique, spacious dining room with separate tables. Ideal for touring the Highlands and many of Scotland's beauty spots by various roads. Ample parking. Personal Scottish attention. Food Hygiene Certificate awarded. Open Easter to beginning of October. Evening Meal, Bed and Breakfast from £17.50 or Bed and Breakfast only from £11.50. Brochure on request.

BRIDGE OF CALLY. Mrs Josephine MacLaren, Blackcraig Castle, Bridge of Cally PH10 7PX (Bridge of Cally [0250] 886251 or 031-551 1863).

Blackcraig Castle, Bridge of Cally, Perthshire

A beautiful castle of architectural interest situated in spacious grounds. Free trout fishing on own stretch of River Ardle. Pony trekking can be arranged. Ideal for family holidays — children especially welcome. Traditional Scottish Fare served in panelled diningroom with separate tables; beautiful drawing-room with log fire. Seven double, two single and three family rooms, eight with washbasins; two bathrooms, four toilets; cot, high chair. Pets permitted. Car essential — parking. Excellent centre for touring — Braemar, Pitlochry (Festival Theatre), Crieff, Dunkeld etc. Open for guests from July to first Sunday in September. Saturday to Saturday booking. Evening Dinner, Night Supper, Bed and Breakfast £130 weekly per person. Reductions for children under 14 years. SAE, please. Enquiries from November to end June to **1 Inverleith Place, Edinburgh EH3 5QE.**

Terms quoted in this publication may be subject to increase if rises in costs necessitate

CALLANDER. Lynne and Alistair Ferguson, Roslin Cottage Guest House, Lagrannoch, Callander FK17 8LE (0877 30638). Situated on the outskirts of Callander, the gateway to the Trossachs, Roslin Cottage has recently been renovated and restored yet still retains many original features including stone walls, beams and an open fireplace in the lounge. We offer a varied Scottish Breakfast using own produce when available and Evening Meals are provided on request. There are tea/coffee-makers in all bedrooms. Excellent area for touring. We like to make our guests feel at home and ensure their stay is enjoyable. Dogs are especially welcome, stay free. Bed and Breakfast from £12.50 to £14 per person per night; four course Evening Meal from £11 per person. Special weekly and fortnightly rates available. Brochure on request.

CAPUTH (Murthly). Mrs Rachel Smith, Stralochy Farm, Caputh, Murthly PH1 4LQ (Caputh [073871] 250). Working farm. This is a modern bungalow situated in a lovely spot, with trees and lochs abounding in the neighbourhood. Central for touring Perthshire and not far from Perth, Dundee and "Bonnie Glenshee". Stralochy is a mixed arable farm with 239 acres of land. One double and one twin bedrooms; bathroom, two toilets; sittingroom and diningroom with electric heating and coal fires. Children are welcome — cot, babysitting by arrangement. Sorry, no pets. Evening Dinner, Bed and Breakfast (reductions for children). Terms on request. Open May to October. Dunkeld four miles, Blairgowrie seven miles, Perth 14 miles and Pitlochry 20. Good food served. Car essential — parking.

COMRIE/CRIEFF. Mr T.A. Griffiths, Mossgiel Guesthouse, Burrell Street, Comrie, Crieff PH6 2JP (0764 70567). 🐾 Picturesque Comrie is set at the foot of the Highlands enjoying spectacular scenery. Ideally situated for Perthshire's many attractions. 20 Golf Courses within easy reach, extensive walking, fishing and hunting. Watersports centre on Loch Earn, ski-ing at Glenshee. You are assured a friendly welcome at Mossgiel Guesthouse. Six double rooms, central heating, tea making facilities. A home from home residents' lounge, colour TV. A hearty Breakfast and three course Dinner menu prepared and home cooked by your hostess. Reductions for children. Pets welcome. Bed and Breakfast from £13.50 to £15; Dinner £7.50.

CRIANLARICH. Mr & Mrs A. Chisholm, Tigh Na Struith, The Riverside Guest House, Crianlarich FK20 8RU (Crianlarich [08383] 235). Voted the Best Guest House in Britain by the British Guild of Travel Writers in 1984, this superbly sited Guest House comprises six bedrooms, each with unrestricted views of the Crianlarich mountains. The three-acre garden leads down to the River Fillan, a tributary of the River Tay. Personally run by the owners, Janice and Sandy Chisholm, Tigh Na Struith allows visitors the chance to relax and enjoy rural Scotland at its best. To this end, each bedroom is centrally heated, double glazed, with colour TV and tea/coffee making facilities. Open March to November. Bed and Breakfast from £16 per person. British Travel Writers "Tops Award" 1984.

DUNKELD. Mrs P.W. Buxton, Bheinne Mhor, Perth Road, Birnam, Dunkeld PH8 0DH (0350 727779). Attractive Victorian detached stone house with private garden and car park, ideally situated for exploring Macbeth's famous Birnam Woods, fishing, golfing or hill walking. Beautiful scenery all around with trees, rivers, hills and lochs; many places of historic interest including Dunkeld Cathedral. Comfortable double, twin, family or single bedrooms, all with washbasins (two en-suite, one with private bathroom), razor points, electric blankets and tea/coffee making facilities. Bathroom, two toilets. Diningroom with separate tables; colour TV lounge. Evening Meal by arrangement. Open all year. A warm welcome awaits guests. Bed and Breakfast from £14 to £18.

DUNKELD by. Mrs J. MacLean, Woodinch House (FHG), Dalguise, By Dunkeld PH8 0JU (0350 727442). Warm welcome to a comfortable family home set in 30 acres of beautiful Perthshire countryside. Bed and Breakfast, Dinner and packed lunches available. One double and one family/twin bedrooms; bathroom with shower. Sittingroom with log fire and TV. Dinner is beautifully prepared and presented (Cordon Bleu) using fresh local produce. Woodinch is very peaceful, situated at the gateway to the Highlands in the Tay Valley, four miles north of Dunkeld off the A9 Perth/Inverness road. Relax and enjoy local amenities such as fishing, pony trekking, golfing, beautiful walks and sightseeing — explore the Highlands. Terms from £12 for Bed and Breakfast; £10 Dinner.

PLEASE ENCLOSE A STAMPED ADDRESSED ENVELOPE WITH ENQUIRIES

MEIGLE. Mr and Mrs Eskdale, Stripside, Longleys, Meigle PH12 8QX (08284 388). Situated in the

quiet of the Strathmore Valley, "Stripside" is close at hand for the ski slopes of Glenshee, fishing, pony trekking and a wide range of golf courses. Our cosy farmhouse is centrally heated with a coal fire for chillier evenings. Drying facilities. All bedrooms are en-suite, have colour TV and tea/coffee making facilities. Open all year. Parking. Sorry, no dogs, but cats can be boarded in our licensed cattery. Bed and Breakfast £15 (£95 weekly); Dinner, Bed and Breakfast £22 (£140 weekly).

PERTH. Mrs Mary Fotheringham, Craighall Farmhouse, Forgandenny, Near Bridge of Earn, Perth PH2 9DF (0738 812415). 🐾🐾 *Commended.* **Working**

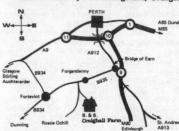

farm. Come and stay in a modern and warm farmhouse with a cheerful, friendly atmosphere situated in lovely Earn Valley, half a mile west of village of Forgandenny on B935 and only six miles south of Perth. True Highland hospitality and large choice for breakfast served in diningroom overlooking fields where a variety of cattle, sheep and lambs graze. Farm produce used. Open all year, the 1000 acre arable and stock farm is within easy reach of Stirling, Edinburgh, St. Andrews, Glasgow and Pitlochry. Fishing, golf, tennis, swimming locally. Hill walking amid lovely scenery. Two rooms with private en-suite facilities, others with washbasins. Double, twin and family rooms. Tea making facilities. Bathroom; sittingroom. Cot, high chair and reduced rates for children. Sorry, no pets. Central heating. Car not essential, public transport 500 yards. Parking. Bed and Breakfast from £13.50. Mid-week bookings taken. AA/RAC acclaimed.

PITLOCHRY. Mrs Ruth MacPherson-McDougall, Dalnasgadh House, Killiecrankie, By Pitlochry PH16 5LN (0796 473237). Attractive country house in

grounds of two acres amidst magnificent Highland scenery. Close to National Trust Centre in Pass of Killiecrankie, historic Blair Castle nearby. Only four miles from Pitlochry with its famous Festival Theatre. Easy touring distance to QUEEN'S VIEW, LOCH TUMMEL, BALMORAL, BRAEMAR, GLAMIS CASTLE, SCONE PALACE and AVIEMORE. Centrally heated throughout. Lounge with colour TV. All bedrooms have washbasins with shaver points, electric blankets and tea/coffee making facilities. Convenient toilets, showers, bathroom. Sorry, no pets. Open Easter to October. AA and RAC Listed. Fire Certificate Awarded. Write, telephone or just call in to enquire terms.

PORT OF MENTEITH. Mrs C. Tough, Collymoon Pendicle, Port of Menteith, By Kippen FK8 3JY (036085 222). 🐾🐾 *Commended.* This large modern

bungalow which sits off the B8043 is an ideal base for touring the Trossachs, Aberfoyle, Callander and Loch Lomond. Sample good home cooking in the newly built sun lounge with panoramic views of the Campsie Hills to the south. Next door is the family farm where you are free to wander and walk along the banks of the River Forth where salmon and brown trout fishing is available. Golf, putting, hill walking, pony trekking all available within eight miles. Trout fishing on Lake of Menteith three miles away. Accommodation comprises one family, one double and one single bedrooms all with tea making facilities, washbasins and shaver points. Cot and high chair provided. Bathroom, toilet and shower facilities. Separate residents' lounge with colour TV. Central heating. Ample parking. Open Easter to October. Sorry no pets. Bed and Breakfast from £12; Evening Dinner £7 per person. Reduced rates for children. Member of STB. AA QQ.

If you've found
FARM HOLIDAY GUIDES
of service please tell your friends

STANLEY. Mrs Ann Guthrie, Newmill Farm, Stanley PH1 4QD (Perth [0738] 828281). This 330-acre farm is situated on the A9, six miles north of Perth. Accommodation comprises twin and double room en-suite, and family rooms available; sitting/diningroom; bathroom, shower room and toilet. Bed and Breakfast from £13; Evening Meal on request. The warm welcome and supper of excellent home baking is inclusive. Reductions and facilities for children. Pets accepted. The numerous castles and historic ruins around Perth are testimony to Scotland's turbulent past. Situated in the area known as "The Gateway to the Highlands" the farm is ideally placed for those seeking some of the best unspoilt scenery in Western Europe. Many famous golf courses and trout rivers in the Perth area. Tourist Board registered.

STRATHYRE. Mrs Catherine B. Reid, Coire Buidhe, Strathyre FK18 8NA (Strathyre [087-74] 288). Run by the longest established hosts in Strathyre, Coire Buidhe sits in the beautiful valley of Strathyre, nine miles from Callander. An excellent base for touring Loch Lomond, Trossachs, Stirling, Edinburgh, with both east and west coasts within easy reach. One single, two twin, three double (one with en-suite bathroom), two family rooms, all with heaters, washbasins, electric blankets, shaver points and tea-making facilities; two showers, bathroom, three toilets. Sitting and diningrooms. Open all year. Parking. Regret, no dogs. Children welcome at reduced terms; cot, high chair, babysitting offered. All water sports and shooting available plus trekking, tennis, hill walking, golf and putting. Bed and Breakfast from £13; Dinner from £8.50. All food personally prepared; home baking. Special diets catered for. Well recommended. Full Fire Certificate. Reduced weekly terms. SAE, please. Tourist Board Approved, Listed.

THORNHILL (by Stirling). Mrs Graham, Mackeanstone House, Doune FK16 6AX (078-685 213). Comfortable country house with relaxed, family atmosphere. One double bedroom with bathroom en-suite, one twin bedroom with private bathroom; sittingroom with TV. Tea/coffee facilities in rooms. Large garden. We are situated at the Gateway to the Highlands, and local attractions include Stirling Castle, Doune Motor Museum, Blair Drummond Safari Park, hill walking in the Trossachs. Pets by arrangement. Children welcome. STB registered. Bed and Breakfast from £15.

ROSS-SHIRE

AULTBEA. Mrs A. MacRae, Mellondale, 47 Mellon Charles, Aultbea IV22 2JL (0445 731326). "Mellondale" is a small family guest house which stands in its own grounds in an acre of garden overlooking Loch Ewe, three miles from the village of Aultbea and nine miles from Inverewe Gardens. Within easy reach of many beautiful beaches, mountains, lochs and nature trails. Excellent area for bird watchers and walkers. Ideal for a quiet restful holiday surrounded by dramatic scenery. Guests are accommodated in four double bedrooms and one twin bedded room, four of which are en-suite. All have colour TV, tea/coffee making facilities, shaver points, electric blankets and duvets. Lounge with TV. Two bathrooms. Diningroom with separate tables where excellent home cooked food is served. Central heating throughout. Parking, car essential. Dinner, Bed and Breakfast. SAE for details.

AULTBEA. Mrs Mairi M. MacNeill, Buena Vista, Aultbea, By Achnasheen IV22 2HU (0445 731374). Guests are welcomed to this modernised croft house in a lovely part of Wester Ross from April to October. The house is situated about quarter-of-a-mile from the main road, surrounded by mountains and overlooking Loch Ewe. There are opportunities for birdwatching, walking, fishing, visiting nearby beaches, tropical gardens, pottery and knitwear shops. Good home cooking, friendly atmosphere. Two double, one twin rooms all with tea-making facilities. Guest bathroom, with shower. Peat fire in diningroom and sun lounge with TV for guests' use. Bed and Breakfast from £13; Dinner, Bed and Breakfast from £20. Pets welcome. Tourist Board registered.

AULTBEA. Mrs Peggy MacRae, "Cove View", 36 Mellon Charles, Aultbea, Wester Ross IV22 2JL
(0445 731 351). Chalet, ideal for quiet relaxing holiday, with lovely views of sea and mountains. Accommodation contains two double bedrooms; bathroom with shower; sittingroom and kitchen alcove. All bed linen supplied. Electric fire. 50p meter. Car essential; ample parking. Inverewe Gardens nine miles away. Open March to November. Bed and Breakfast from £13; Dinner (optional) £10.

AULTBEA. Mrs H. MacLeod, The Croft, Aultbea IV22 2JA (0445 731 352). Guests are assured of a warm welcome at The Croft which stands on its own just yards away from the sea and the village of Aultbea, overlooking Loch Ewe and the Torridon Hills. Lots of hill walking and climbing within easy reach and Inverewe sub-tropical gardens are only five miles away. Unrestricted access and guests are provided with own keys. One twin, one family and one double rooms, all with washbasins and tea-making facilities; bathroom, toilet; sitting/diningroom. All modern conveniences. Cot and babysitting for children. Pets by arrangement only. Car essential — parking. Open from March to October for Bed and Breakfast from £14 minimum; Dinner, Bed and Breakfast from £22.

DIABAIG, WESTER ROSS. Mrs B. Peacock, Upper Diabaig Farm, Diabaig, By Torridon IV22 2HE (044 581 227). Small farmhouse sitting beside trout lochs in bowl of Torridon Hills, offers warm welcome, comfortable accommodation (double/twin/single) all with washbasins and tea making facilities. Ample hot water for bath/shower. Traditional sittingroom with open peat fires early/late season. Separate diningroom. Good home cooking and baking. Local produce in season. Ideal walking, fishing in sea or hill lochs or bird watching. Come and enjoy the peace and quiet of an unspoilt area. Opportunity (in season) to see hand milking, peat cutting, sheep shearing and bottle fed lambs. Open Easter to end September. Bed and Breakfast from £13.50; Dinner available on request.

LOCHCARRON. Mrs D. Rore, A'chomraich, Lochcarron IV54 8YD (05202 225). This 100 year old modernised house stands in a quiet location, by the lochside, in the picturesque village of Lochcarron. The accommodation consists of one double and one twin bedroom, each with washbasin; lounge and diningroom. Bed and Breakfast from £12.50. Lochcarron is an excellent centre for the walker and lover of wildlife and is centrally situated for those wishing to visit Skye, Torridon and Inverewe. Further details on request.

LOCHCARRON WEST (Wester Ross). Mrs Flora Catto, The Creagan, West Lochcarron IV54 8YH (Lochcarron [052-02] 430). 🐝 *Commended.* A warm Highland welcome awaits visitors to this attractive bungalow overlooking Loch Carron, with all bedrooms on the ground floor. Private lounge and bathroom for guests' use only. Central heating in all rooms. One double and one family rooms with washbasin and tea-making facilities. Children welcome, babysitting. Pets accepted free of charge. Sea 40 yards. Ideal touring centre — within easy reach of Inverewe Gardens, three-quarters of an hour from Isle of Skye and Kintail; one and a half hours from Inverness and Easter Ross. Golf course, Torridon Nature Reserve, hill walks, plenty of hill lochs for trout fishing. Car essential — parking. Open April to October for Evening Dinner, Bed and Breakfast from £18 per person; Bed and Breakfast from £12. Reduced rates for children. Scottish Tourist Board registered.

POOLEWE. Mrs K. MacDonald, "Benlair", Near Cove, Poolewe IV22 2LS (0445 86 354). 🐝 *Commended.* Family run cottage situated in tranquil setting with superb views over the sea, 200 yards from sandy beach, near village of Cove. Tea/coffee making facilities in both bedrooms. Farm Holiday Guide Award Winner. Bed and Breakfast from £20 per person per night. Dogs welcome at small charge.

TAIN. Andrew and Nicky Arthur, The Sycamores, Balintore, Tain IV20 1XW (0862 832322). 🐝🐝

Commended. Enjoy a warm welcome at our friendly, family farm by the Moray Firth. There are horses and Highland cattle, calves and piglets to feed and eggs to collect. Relax in our comfortable house or try the local activities — golf, pony trekking, bird watching and fishing are all available. Visit distilleries, gardens and castles, or stroll down to the village with its sandy beaches. Children are always welcome, as we have a young family ourselves. The bedrooms are well-appointed with private facilities and are on the ground floor for easy access. We are a non-smoking house. Open all year. Bed and Breakfast £15; Dinner, Bed and Breakfast £25.

ULLAPOOL. Mrs Isobel Renwick, Clachan Farm, Lochbroom, Ullapool IV23 2RZ (0854 85 209).

🐝🐝 *Commended.* Excellent accommodation is provided in this very comfortable modern farmhouse, seven miles south of Ullapool and two minutes from the A835. Under one hour from Inverness. Three course breakfast, electric blankets, TV lounge available all day. The area has walking, climbing, birdwatching, loch and sea fishing and pleasure cruising. The exotic Inverewe Gardens, Corrieshalloch Gorge and Nature Reserves are all within easy reach. No smoking household. No Sunday enquiries. Bed and Breakfast. Open Easter to November.

ROXBURGHSHIRE

HAWICK near. Mrs Mary Jackson, "Colterscleugh", Teviothead, Hawick TD9 0LF (0450-85-247). Situated just off the A7 Carlisle to Hawick road in Border country, "Colterscleugh" is open to guests all year round. Within easy reach of many historic buildings, museums and Border castles. Pleasant walks and pony trekking locally; fishing nearby. Golf and sporting facilities in Hawick. Woollens and cashmere are made here and visits to the various mills can be arranged. Comfortable bedrooms. Bathroom, two toilets; sittingroom with TV, diningroom. Pets allowed. Parking. Public transport a few yards away. Reduced rates for children. Bed, Breakfast and Evening Meal available. Further details gladly supplied. Please send SAE.

HAWICK. Mrs Sheila Shell, Wiltonburn Farm, Hawick TD9 7LL (0450 72414/78000). Wiltonburn is a

friendly, working, mixed farm situated in a sheltered valley and surrounded by fields, hills and a small stream. Relax in the garden, or use the local facilities, including fishing, riding, swimming, golf, squash, tennis or hill walking. An ideal base for visiting castles, museums and stately homes or for buying knitwear. Good selection of eating places nearby. Open all year. Family room en-suite, shower available. Two bathrooms. TV lounge, and garden with furniture and barbecue. Dogs by arrangement. Cot available. Listed Commended. Bed and full Scottish Breakfast from £14. Two self catering units also available.

KELSO. Mr & Mrs A. Stewart, Cliftonhill Farm, Ednam, Kelso TD5 7QE (0573 225028). ₩₩

Cliftonhill is a working family farm in the Scottish Borders. It is situated amidst beautiful and tranquil countryside with panoramic views towards Cheviot and Eildon Hills. The River Eden meanders through the farm to the River Tweed, attracting much wildlife. Ideal for fishing, swimming and walking. Kelso is a picturesque market town with a cobbled square and many sites of historical interest — Floors Castle, Melrose and Kelso Abbeys, Mellerstain House, Marderston. Berwick-upon-Tweed (with lovely beaches) is 16 miles away. There are three bedrooms, all furnished to a high standard; one double with private bathroom, two twin-bedded rooms with a bathroom between them on a separate floor. All rooms with tea making facilities. Delightful farmhouse breakfasts with freshly home made bread. Comfortable lounge with TV. Extensive gardens. Terms from £12 to £16. **There are also three PICTURESQUE, ROMANTIC COTTAGES available on the farm.** Further details on request.

STIRLINGSHIRE

PORT OF MENTEITH. Mrs Norma Erskine, Inchie Farm, Port of Menteith, Stirling FK8 3JZ (087-75 233). ₩₩ *Commended.* Family farm situated on the shores of the beautiful Lake of Menteith, where ospreys nest between April and September. Featured in previous "Wish You Were Here" TV programme. Comfortable twin/family rooms, both with washbasins and tea/coffee making facilities. Shower in bathroom. Central heating throughout. Guests' own TV lounge. An ideal base for touring or hillwalking in nearby Trossachs. Trout fishing can be arranged. Good food well presented using farm produce. Open April to October. Bed and Breakfast from £12 per person; Dinner, Bed and Breakfast from £19 per person.

STIRLING. Mrs Joyce Love, Mia-Roo, 37 Snowdon Place, Stirling FK8 2JP (Stirling [0786] 473979). A large 19th century stone-built house in residential area near town centre, golf course, castle. Central situation makes for easy access to truly picturesque areas of Scotland — the Trossachs, Loch Lomond, Perthshire etc. Less than an hour from Edinburgh, Glasgow, St. Andrews and Perth. Over 30 golf courses within 30 mile radius including Gleneagles. Stirling Castle and other National Trust properties easily accessible. Twin/double, family and single rooms with hot and cold washbasins and shaver points. There is a large lounge and diningroom. Unrestricted access. Stirling, Loch Lomond and Trossachs Tourist Board registered. Bed and Breakfast from £14.50 per person. Special rates for children.

STIRLING by. Mrs Grace M. Findlay, Easter Tarr Farm, Thornhill, By Stirling FK8 3QL (Thornhill [078-685] 225). Working farm. Easter Tarr is an old farmhouse with a homely atmosphere, set in a pretty garden on a 250-acre mixed farm. The region is steeped in history and the scenery is beautiful here on the fringes of the Trossachs. Edinburgh one hour's drive away; Safari Park and Loch Lomond Bear Park nearby. Mrs Findlay gives personal attention and menu includes home made soups, varied main course and delicious sweets. Accommodation in two double and one twin-bedded rooms; bathroom, toilet; sitting-room/diningroom. There is a colour TV in the lounge for visitors' use. Children at reduced rates, cots, high chair and babysitting. Open fire in sittingroom when required. Open March to October inclusive. Bed and Breakfast from £11 to £12; optional Dinner on request. Car essential, parking. SAE, please, for further information. Tourist Board member.

SUTHERLAND

BRORA. Mr and Mrs C.H. Berthelot, Ard Beag, Badnellan, Brora KW9 6NQ (Brora [0408] 621398).

Situated between Inverness and John O' Groats, one mile from the Railway Station and the village of Brora, Ard Beag is a small, comfortable house with spectacular views over the Moray Firth. Brora has fine sandy beaches and is an ideal base for bird-watching, hill walking and touring. Dunrobin Castle and Loch Fleet Nature Reserve are popular attractions. Inverness with Motorail services 56 miles, John O' Groats 67 miles. At Ard Beag all bedrooms (one double, one twin and one single) have sea views, washbasins and electric kettles. Central heating. Home baked bread and excellent home cooking with fresh fruit and vegetables from the garden served when available. Children welcome at reduced rates. Sorry, no pets. Open May to September otherwise with advance booking. Bed and Breakfast from £12; Dinner by arrangement. Dinner, Bed and Breakfast from £20. Reduced weekly terms. Also available, two large six-berth self-catering caravans from £80 weekly, inclusive. Advance bookings advisable.

ROGART. Mrs Johan Corbett, "Benview", Morness, Rogart IV28 3XG (04084 222).

Traditional country farmhouse offering peace and quiet, comfort, good food and friendly, personal attention. Accommodation comprises three bedrooms with tea-making facilities; shower and bathroom; conservatory and smoking lounge, TV lounge and dining room. Full central heating. An ideal base for day trips to the north, west and east coasts. Also ideal for hill walking, golfing, fishing, wildlife, bird watching. Children over five years welcome. Dogs by arrangement. Bed and Breakfast from £13.50; Dinner from £6. Reduced rates for children. Open May to October. STB Listed "Commended".

WIGTOWNSHIRE

NEWTON STEWART. Miss K.R. Wallace, Kiloran, 6 Auchendoon Road, Newton Stewart DG8 6HD (Newton Stewart [0671] 2818).

Spacious, luxury bungalow set in secluded landscaped garden, with panoramic views of Galloway Hills, in quiet area of Newton Stewart. Enjoy comfortable accommodation on one level in two double bedrooms (one twin-bedded); bathroom with shower; cloakroom with WC. Soap and towels supplied. Lounge (colour TV), diningroom where good home cooking is served (menu changed daily). Central heating. Children over 10 years welcome. Dogs allowed, but not in house. Ideal centre for touring Galloway. Safe, sandy beaches 12 miles. Within easy reach of hill walking, golf, riding and trekking. Terms on request, SAE, please, for Evening Dinner, Bed and Breakfast or Bed and Breakfast only. For Auchendoon Road, turn at Dashwood Square to Princess Road, then second on right. Ample parking available. Tourist Board member.

SCOTTISH ISLANDS

ISLE OF ARRAN

WHITING BAY. Peter and Barbara Rawlin, **View Bank Guest House, Golf Course Road, Whiting Bay KA27 8QT (077-07-326).** ✿ ✿ *Commended.*

View Bank Guest House is set in three-quarters of an acre of garden with superb views over Firth of Clyde. An old attractive farmhouse, modernised throughout, with central heating and log burning fires. A friendly, homely place offering good home cooking. Two double, three family, one twin and one single bedrooms (one room en-suite); sittingroom; diningroom; bathroom; shower room; three toilets. Children welcome. Cot and babysitting on request. Pets by arrangement. Excellent 18-hole golf course at £5 per round. Most sporting activities available: diving, pony trekking, tennis, etc plus craft activities: spinning, weaving. Beautiful walks with sea only 400 yards away. Bed and Breakfast from £14.50; Dinner, Bed and Breakfast from £21.50. Reductions for children. TWICE WINNERS OF FARM HOLIDAY GUIDE DIPLOMA.

ISLE OF IONA

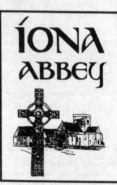
ISLE OF MULL

LOCH DON, near Craignure. Mrs Sheila Campbell, **Redburn, Loch Don, Near Craignure PA64 6AP (Craignure [068-02] 370).** Redburn is a newly renovated Croft House situated in half an acre on the side of Loch Don, four miles from Craignure. The three bedrooms (one double and two twin) have en-suite and tea/coffee making facilities. Home cooking is a speciality. The area is ideal for bird watchers and natural history enthusiasts and there are drying facilities for outdoor clothing. There is access to sitting/diningroom at all times. Dinner, Bed and Breakfast from £25 to £26. Bed and Breakfast from £15. Further details available on request.

ORKNEYS

RACKWICK. Mrs D.A. Rendall, "Glen", Rackwick, Hoy KW16 3NJ (085679 262). Nearest accommodation to the Old Man of Hoy. Farmhouse Bed and Breakfast (dinner optional) on small hill farm. Splendid views across the Pentland Firth. One twin room with shower and washbasin, one double. From £12. Also self catering châlet, fully furnished. Two bedrooms — double and twin. Shower room with WC and washbasin. Kitchen-cum-sittingroom with Gaz cooker, sink, fridge, colour TV. Electricity extra. Bed linen and towels not provided. From £70 to £100 per week. Wee Cottage sleeps two/three. Fully furnished. All electric, storage heaters; Baby Belling cooker. Bedroom; kitchen-cum-sittingroom; shower room with toilet and washbasin. From £70 to £100 per week.

WESTRAY. Cleaton House Hotel, Westray KW17 2DB (085 77 508). Welcome to "The Jewel of the Isles". Cleaton House is centrally located and as such is the ideal base from which to explore the castles, cliffs and beaches of Westray. Our menu incorporates local produce wherever possible, especially beef, shellfish and fresh vegetables. A la carte licensed restaurant and supper room. All rooms are not only spacious and comfortable but also have panoramas of land and sea. Courtesy bus from airfield and ferries. Bicycle hire.

ISLE OF RAASAY

RAASAY. Isle of Raasay Hotel, Raasay, By Kyle of Lochalsh, Ross-shire IV40 8PB (047-862 222). 👑 👑 👑 *Commended.* Warm hospitality, personal service, magnificent views over the sea to Skye — this and much more awaits you at this delightful hotel on the historic and unspoilt island of Raasay. Ideally situated for hill walking, birdwatching, fishing and field trips. Enjoy fresh local produce and home baking in our dining room overlooking the Narrows of Raasay. 12 bedrooms — one single, nine twin and two double — all with private facilities. Open from Easter to mid October.

ISLE OF SKYE

KYLEAKIN. Mrs E. MacLennan, 16 Kyleside, Kyleakin IV41 8PW (0599 4468). Bed and Breakfast, Evening Meal if required. Highly recommended for home cooking and baking. Central heating. All rooms have hot and cold washbasins and tea/coffee making facilities. Fire Certificate held. Set among magnificent scenery overlooking the sea and Lochalsh. Only a five minute ferry crossing.

Neidpath Castle, an early Fraser stronghold, situated on the banks of the River Tweed near Peebles.

SELF-CATERING HOLIDAYS

ABERDEENSHIRE

HUNTLY by. Logie Newton Holiday Cottages, By Huntly. 🌼 🌼 🌼 🌼 *Commended.* **Cottages sleep 4/6 plus cot.** Two cottages (one two bedroomed the other three bedroomed) in Whisky and Castle country on the working family farm of Logie Newton, eight miles east of Huntly. Recently refurbished to a high standard yet retaining their traditional character and charm. Warmth, cleanliness, comfort and Scottish hospitality our priority. Ideal central base for touring north east Scotland with a variety of sporting facilities nearby. Within one hour's drive of Royal Deeside, Speyside, Aberdeen and coastal fishing villages. Children and well behaved pets welcome. Open all year. £125 to £300 weekly. Details from **Mrs R. Cruickshank, Logie Newton, By Huntly AB54 6BB (04644 229; Fax: 04644 277).**

Forglen HOLIDAY COTTAGES

AWAY FROM IT ALL

For brochure contact:
The Secretary,
HOLIDAY COTTAGES,
Forglen Estate, Turriff, Aberdeenshire AB53 7JP
Tel: (0888) 62918

The Estate lies along the beautiful Deveron River and our traditional stone cottages (modernised and well equipped) nestle in individual seclusion. Visitors are free to wander and explore one of the ancient baronies of Scotland. The sea is only nine miles away, and the market town of Turriff only 2 miles, with its golf course, swimming pool, etc. Many places of interest including the Cairngorms, Aviemore, picturesque fishing villages and castles, all within easy reach on uncrowded roads. Horse riding. See our wildlife and Highland cattle.

STB 🌼 **Approved to** 🌼 🌼 **Commended**
Terms: £60 to £260 weekly, including VAT and firewood
Special Winter lets. Electricity by coin meter.
11 cottages sleeping 6-8.
Children and reasonable dogs welcome.

PLEASE ENCLOSE A STAMPED ADDRESSED ENVELOPE WITH ENQUIRIES

ANGUS

ABERLEMNO. Mrs C. Spence, Balglassie, Aberlemno, By Forfar DD8 3PH (030 783 208; changing Spring 1993 to 0307 830208). ❦❦❦ *Commended.*

Working farm. Comfortable bungalow sleeps six in three bedrooms (four single beds, one double) and cottage sleeps five in two bedrooms (three single beds, one double). Situated on a mixed working farm. Well equipped accommodation incorporates lounge/diningroom, kitchen, bathroom. Colour TV, heating all rooms. Balglassie Farm is situated four miles from Brechin, eight miles from Forfar. The South Esk flows by and fishing or pleasant walks can be enjoyed. Situated within easy reach of the Angus glens, sea and recreational facilities, this is an ideal touring centre. Golfing, bowling, pony trekking, riding, nature reserve and walks all nearby. Available January to December. Weekly rates from £90 to £170. Electricity by 50p meter. Linen not provided but can be hired by request. Salmon and sea trout fishing £5 daily.

ARGYLL

**If you've found
FARM HOLIDAY GUIDES
of service please tell your friends**

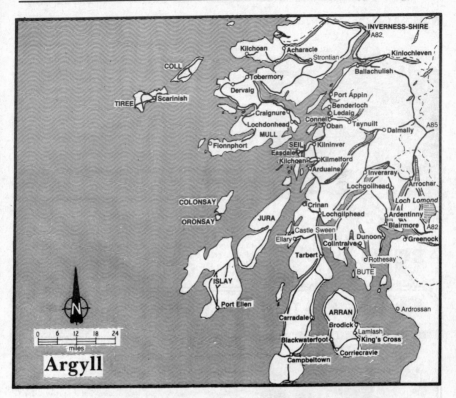

APPIN. Glencreran Estate, Appin. Lodge sleeps 14, Farmhouse sleeps 8/9. In quiet glen, magnificent scenery. 20 miles Oban, 30 miles Fort William. Car essential. Mains electricity. Heating by storage heaters/oil/log fires. Walking, climbing, fishing, sailing, riding in the vicinity. Shops seven miles. Steamer trips, golf, swimming pool in Oban and Fort William. Weekly rates inclusive of VAT £345 to £670. Details from **D.M. Harrison, Scottish Argicultural College, Glencruitten Road, Oban PA34 4DW (0631 63093; Fax: 0631 65074).**

APPIN. Ardtur Cottages, Appin. Two adjacent cottages in secluded surroundings on promontory between Port Appin and Castle Stalker, opposite north end of Isle of Lismore. Ideal centre for hill walking, climbing, etc. (Glen Coe and Ben Nevis half-hour drive). Direct access across the field to sea (Loch Linnhe). Tennis court available by arrangement, also hire of bicycles. Boat hire, pony trekking, fly fishing all available locally. Accommodation in first cottage for eight people in four double bedrooms, large dining/sittingroom/kitchenette and two bathrooms. Second cottage accommodates six people im three twin bedded rooms, dining/sittingroom, kitchenette and bathroom. Everything is provided except linen. Shops one mile; sea 200 yards. Pets allowed. Car essential, parking. Open March/October. SAE, please, for terms to **Mrs J. Pery, Ardtur, Appin PA38 4DD (063-173 223 or 0626 834172).**

ARDTUR COTTAGES

BALVICAR (near Oban). Mr Ross Macaskill, Balvicar Farm, Balvicar Chalets, By Oban PA34 4TE (Balvicar [085-23] 221). 🏵🏵🏵🏵 *Commended.*

Working farm. Chalets sleep 4. This seven chalet site has spectacular views across sea to mountains beyond. Balvicar is 15 miles from Oban which is an excellent motor-touring centre as well as the starting point for steamer and boat trips to many islands. Chalets are all-electric with two bedrooms, bathroom, kitchen/lounge. Laundry room with washing machine and dryer. Fully furnished for four persons, continental quilts, colour TV, boat available. Shop one mile. Eating out facilities three miles. The area is ideal for walking, bird watching, sailing. Open March to November. Weekly prices from £110 to £250 per chalet. Discounts for two adults or for fortnightly bookings.

CAMPBELTOWN. Colonel and Mrs W.T.C. Angus, Kilchrist Castle, Campbeltown PA28 6PH (Campbeltown [0586] 553210). 🏵🏵 and 🏵🏵🏵

KILCHRIST CASTLE

Commended. **Cottages sleep 2/6 adults.** Six small, cosy, nicely modernised, bright, comfortably furnished, fully-equipped self-contained cottages for two to six people in the 13-acre grounds of Kilchrist Castle, near Campbeltown and the famous Mull of Kintyre. Colour TV and bed linen included, but not towels or table linen. All electric, with microwave, electric convector heaters and coal-effect fires. Meet Lachie, Gabrielle and their daughter Loretta, our black Shetland ponies. Maybe encounter Billeonie, our fabled kindly Kilchrist brownie at his wishing well at the Old Byre of Kilchrist. Laundry room with automatic washing machine and tumble dryer. Personally supervised by the proprietors, Colonel and Mrs W.T.C. Angus. Terms £155 to £285. SAE appreciated.

See also Colour Display Advertisement

CAMPBELTOWN by. Mrs Nickerson, Cour, By Campbeltown PA28 6QL (Skipness [088-06] 236/233). Properties sleep 2/12. Cour is a private estate on the east coast of Kintyre, nine miles north of Carradale, remote but not isolated. Two houses, one annexe and four cottages, formerly the homes of estate workers, accommodating from two to twelve, all electric, well-equipped, cot; launderette at farm. Private beach, boats, good sea fishing. Trout fishing, badminton and ping-pong — no extra charge. Ideal area for walking and touring. Car essential — parking. Pets accepted. Shopping at Carradale or Skipness. Open all year. SAE, please, for brochure.

COLINTRAIVE BY. Maymore Farm, Glendaruel, By Colintraive, Argyll. Sleeps 9 plus baby. Self catering in five bedrooms for nine plus baby. Situated one

mile from village on quiet open road. Estuary of River Ruel four miles. Views to hills and fields, no near neighbours. Lovely spot for peaceful holiday also convenient touring base. Loch Lomond and Inveraray 30 miles, Oban and Glencoe 50 miles. An ideal family house with walled garden and though not modern quite comfortably equipped. Large living/diningroom, sittingroom with log fire and TV. Kitchen; bathroom. Two single, two double, one triple bedrooms plus cot. Fully equipped except for linen. Open May to October. Please send SAE mentioning dates being considered to **Mrs S. MacKellar, Ardacheranmor, Glendaruel, By Colintraive, Argyll PA22 3AE (036982 209).**

STRATHCLYDE REGION – WHERE TO START?

Scotland's most densely populated region houses more people than many small countries. At its centre is Glasgow where you will find many attractions including the Art Gallery and the Burrell Collection. Heading further out this Region includes such popular places as Oban, the Mull of Kintyre, the Clyde Valley, the Ayrshire Coast and Argyll Forest Park.

See also Colour Display Advertisement **CRINAN. Mike Murray, Kilmahumaig, Crinan, By Lochgilphead PA31 8SW (Crinan [054-683] 238). ♛ ♛ ♛** *Commended.* **Flats sleep 2/6.** Kilmahumaig Barns provide three self-contained flats accommodating two/six in one or two bed-roomed units. Kilmahumaig nestles in the hills that form the promontory of Crinan, one of the most attractive locations on the West Coast and the entrance to the famous Crinan Canal, with its constant activity of yachts and fishing boats. This is an ideal place for all the usual country pursuits and just what you need for a truly relaxing holiday. Member of Association of Scotland's Self Caterers. Terms from £60 to £230.

CRINAN FERRY. The Ferryman's Cottage, Crinan Ferry, Lochgilphead. ♛ ♛ ♛ ♛ *Commended.* **Sleeps 6.** The Ferryman's Cottage is situated on the end of a peninsula overlooking Crinan Moss and is surrounded by sandy beaches and spectacular views. It is a paradise for children and bird-watchers. The traditional stone cottage sleeps six in three bedrooms. There is an all-electric kitchen, wood panelled sittingroom with open fire, diningroom and a bathroom. The cottage is comfortable and charming. Duvets with covers are provided, but not linen. Tourist Board registered. SAE for details to **Mrs Rachel Walker, The Change House, Crinan Ferry, Lochgilphead PA31 8QH (Kilmartin [054-65] 232).**

DALMALLY by. Mrs D. Fellowes, Inistrynich, By Dalmally PA33 1BQ (Dalmally [083-82] 256). Two

cottages situated on a private estate surrounded by beautiful scenery. Garden Cottage (four bedrooms) and Inistrynich Cottage (two bedrooms). Situated five miles from Dalmally, 11 miles from Inveraray, 28 miles from Oban, the cottages overlook Loch Awe and each has a garden. They are furnished to a high standard with heaters in all rooms and an open fire in the livingroom. Both have electric cookers, fridge, immersion heater, electric kettle, iron, hoover, washing machine and colour TV. Cot and high chair available on request. Linen not provided. Dogs allowed by arrangement. Car essential — ample parking space. Ideal centre for touring mainland and Western Isles. Good restaurants, hill walking, forest walks, fishing, boat trips, pony trekking all within easy reach. SAE, please, for brochure and terms.

Peace and Quiet at Rockhill Farm

Two comfortable farm cottages, each sleeping a maximum of six persons. Everything provided except linen. Cot available. Situated on Rockhill Farm, 150 yards from the loch shore with wonderful views of the Loch and Ben Cruachan. Guests may bring their own boat and take their car to shore, or hire a boat and engine. Parking outside the door. We breed Hanoverian horses and also sheep. Each cottage has a kitchen, bathroom with shower, bath and toilets, and large living/dining room overlooking the Loch. Electric cooker and kettle, electric fires or radiators in all rooms, fridge freezer and microwave, spin dryer, immersion heater, hoover, toaster and colour TV. Ideal for touring Argyll or for a quiet holiday on the farm. Places of interest include Inveraray, Glencoe, Cruachan, Oban and Loch Etive for boat trips. Forest walks, horse riding, pony trekking, hill walking. Car essential. Dogs by arrangement. SAE please, for brochure and terms which include free trout fishing.

Helen and Brian Whalley, Rockhill Farm Country House, Ardbrecknish, by Dalmally, Argyll PA33 1BH. Tel: [086-63] 218

Mr & Mrs E. Crawford, Blarghour Farm, Lochaweside, by Dalmally Argyll PA33 1BW   Tel: Kilchrenan (086-63) 246

RELAX at any season in the comfort of a centrally heated, double glazed, tastefully appointed holiday home on a working hill farm.

ABSORB the peaceful atmosphere of unspoiled, natural suroundings with abundant wildlife.

APPRECIATE the superb views of loch and mountain which each property commands.

ENJOY hill-walking, bird watching, fishing, boating and touring.

VISIT the 90 foot waterfall on the farm and castles and gardens locally.

SELECT your holiday "home from home", from houses sleeping eight, four and two and a bungalow sleeping five, each fully carpeted, tastefully decorated, comfortably furnished and well appointed with fridge/freezer, washer/dryer, telephone, colour television and garden furniture. Bed linen is supplied and beds made up for your arrival.

🏵🏵🏵🏵 Deluxe
🏵🏵🏵🏵 Highly Commended

COLOUR BROCHURE ON REQUEST.

Please see our colour advertisement on page 6.

Sonachan House Self-catering Holidays
★ **Luxury Period Apartments**
★ **Large detached Burn-side Cottage**
★ **Traditional Chalets**   ★**Loch-side Caravans**
🏵🏵🏵🏵 COMMENDED to HIGHLY COMMENDED

Sonachan is a beautifully situated loch-side mansion-house (formerly a hunting lodge), in lovely grounds and gardens, with breath-taking views across Loch Awe to the mountains. Here you can really unwind and relax – it is exceptionally tranquil. The light is clear, the air is pure and the water is peaty! Simply sit by the loch and soak up the atmosphere. Or if you're energetic, you can go rowing, cycling, swimming, take out a motor boat, play badminton or a gentle game of croquet; even practise your swing in the golf nets. The adventurers may wish to go hill-walking, perhaps take the ferry from Oban to Mull or Iona, or explore ruined castles.

It is a fisherman's paradise (shore fishing is free) with trout, pike, perch, char or the occasional salmon being the main species. (We can arrange fly-fishing tuition or a ghillie). There are indoor games rooms if it rains. We also have a tuckshop, laundry and payphone and will arrange groceries delivery for your arrival. We also offer private Loch Cruises and a ferry service to the nearby Licensed Hotels.

All accommodation has full bed-linen and colour TV. Rates are from £115 to £440 per week and include VAT.

Full Colour Brochure (stamp please):
JONATHAN and JANE SOAR,
Sonachan House, Portsonachan,
By Dalmally, Argyll PA33 1BN.
Telephone: 08663 240.
Fax: 08663 241.

See also Colour Display Advertisement **EASDALE. "Misty Isles", Easdale, Seil Island. Sleeps 2. NON SMOKERS.** In a row of harbourside cottages, this cosy studio cottage has replaced one of the original buildings. The famous village of Easdale, 16 miles south of Oban, is on Seil Island, reached by the only "Bridge over the Atlantic" and has a post office, hotel, gift/craft shops. There are many coach and sea trips available from Oban. It is also a good area for walking and sea fishing. There is private mooring; because of the steep drop we do not accept children. Pets by arrangement. Open-plan living/sleeping/kitchen area, pine panelled throughout, double glazed, hall and bathroom (bath/shower). There are two single divan beds which can be pushed together to form large double bed. Cooking and lighting by electricity (50p meter). Free night storage heating and coal for multi-fuel stove, fridge and colour TV. Rates from £100 to £225 per week. For details please send SAE to **Hank and Maureen Clare, Harbour Cottage, Ellenabeich, Seil Island, By Oban PA34 4RQ (08523 424; answering machine at certain times).**

EASDALE (near Oban). Mrs Helen Simcox, Seaview, Easdale, By Oban PA34 4RG (08523 222). Sleeps 2/4. Cross the famous "Bridge over the Atlantic", 16 miles south of Oban to the picturesque conservation village of Ellenabeich and stay in a traditional white-painted slate quarrier's cottage, skilfully converted to retain its original character. Full gas central heating. Bathroom with shower and fully fitted kitchen with microwave oven. Colour TV. Ample parking. All linen provided. Open all year. Also similar cottage available, sleeps two. The village has ample shops including post office and grocery store. Take a short walk to the Hotel which is open to non-residents and enjoy its excellent "food fayre" and "pub grub". Terms on request.

INVERARAY. Kilblaan Farmhouse, Inveraray. Sleeps 8. A Victorian farmhouse situated in a beautiful glen close to Loch Fyne with lovely views down the glen and to the hills behind. Within close distance of Inveraray, but a car is essential. Wonderful hill walks and bird watching, sea and trout fishing locally. The house offers comfortable accommodation. Sleeps eight with two downstairs bedrooms, sittingroom, large country kitchen with fridge/freezer, cloakroom. Upstairs two bedrooms and bathroom. Part oil heating, part night storage. A well kept garden safe for animals. Car parking. Open March — October. SAE to **Mrs MacLean, Brickmakers Cottage, Lambourn Woodlands, Newbury, Berkshire RG16 7TS (0488 71474).**

See also Colour Display Advertisement **INVERARAY near. Mr and Mrs D. Crawford, Brenchoille Farm, Inveraray PA32 8XN (Furnace [04995] 662).** 🐦🐦🐦 *Commended. Working farm.* Houses sleep 6. Braleckan, a mid-19th century stone building, comprises three houses, fully modernised and equipped to a high standard of comfort. All electric. Carpets throughout and welcoming old-style fires in sitting rooms. Colour TV and payphone. Kitchens have electric cooker, microwave oven, washer/dryer, fridge, kettle, toaster, iron, vacuum cleaner and immersion heater. Bedrooms fully furnished. Bathrooms include heaters and shaver points. Cots and high chairs available. Large parking area. Regretfully no pets. Situated peacefully on hill farm, yet within easy reach of A83 leading to many attractions including nearby Auchindrain Museum and Crarae Gardens. Open all year. Special winter rates. Charges inclusive of linen and VAT. SAE, please, or phone for details.

Please mention this guide when you write or phone to enquire about accommodation.

If you are writing, a stamped, addressed envelope is always appreciated.

ISLE OF LISMORE. Calgary, Laggan, Isle of Lismore. Sleeps 4/5. Modern single storey centrally heated house. Close to sea, facing up the Great Glen to Ben Nevis, overlooking delightful Port Ramsay harbour. Excellent anchorage. Lismore is a fascinating island well known for its pleasant walks, historical sites, wild birds and flowers. Accommodation comprises lounge with colour TV; large kitchen/dining area; shower room with handbasin and WC; two bedrooms with handbasins. Linen supplied. Lismore is served by a car ferry from Oban and a passenger ferry from Port Appin. Taxi service available on the island. Weekly terms from £150 to £240. SAE to **D.A. Livingstone, Calgarry, Laggan, Isle of Lismore PA34 5UN (063176 284/5).**

See also Colour Display Advertisement

KILMARTIN. Susan Malcolm, Duntrune Castle, Kilmartin PA31 8QQ (054-65283). ❀❀❀❀ *Highly Commended.* **Sleep 3/5.** Traditional stone-built cottages on a 5,000 acre estate have their own individual character and private garden. All recently modernised, attractively furnished, fully equipped with wood-burning stoves or open fires, fridges, spin dryers, tumble dryers and duvets; home cooked meals are available on the premises. Loch Crinan provides an ideal setting for a peaceful holiday without being too remote — historical interest, wildlife and outstanding scenery. Hill walking, bird watching and fishing abound; other nearby activities include pony trekking, golf, boating and water sports. Excellent eating-out places locally. SAE requested or telephone for further details.

KILMELFORD. Melfort Village, Kilmelford, By Oban PA34 4XD (08522 257; Fax: 08522 321). Luxury traditional cottages, beautifully modernised and furnished, sleeping between four and ten persons. Melfort Village enjoys superb, unhindered views down Loch Melfort, one of Scotland's most attractive sea lochs. The nearest village (one-and-a-half miles) has a well-stocked shop and post office. We are only 16 miles from Oban, the "Gateway to the Highlands", with its shops, entertainments and ferries to the islands. We have our own private INDOOR SWIMMING POOL, SAUNA, SOLARIUM, GAMES ROOMS as well as a Bar and Restaurant and small Trekking Centre on site. Watersports, bike hire and fishing all available locally. All cottages have fridge, dishwasher, cooker and hob, microwave, colour TV and video. All linen, sheets, duvets, towels provided. Laundry on site. Weekly terms from £205.

KILMICHAEL GLEN. Mr and Mrs D.W. Bracey, Kirnan Estate, Kilmichael Glen, By Kilmartin PA31 8QL (0546 605217). ❀❀❀/❀❀❀❀ *Commended/ Highly Commended.* Three tastefully furnished cottages in single-storey wing of lovely country house (originally a shooting lodge) set in 650 acres in beautiful scenic glen near magnificent Loch Awe and the famous Crinan Canal and harbour. Sleep 7, 2/4 and 2 respectively. Central heating and electric heating. Fridges; TV; laundry room with washing machine and tumble dryer. Kirnan occupies a delightful setting, and offers peace and quiet in outstanding scenery. Much historical interest and many sporting activities including stalking, riding, sailing and golf. Excellent eating-out places locally. Please telephone for brochure.

KILNINVER, by Oban. Set between two working farms, standing at the head of Loch Scammadale (free fishing to residents). Only 20 minutes by car from Oban, Bragleenbeg is ideal for Highland holidays. Situated in mountain and farmland, the house is surrounded by magnificent scenery and wildlife. Part of the house is converted to offer two spacious self-contained flats. Flat One sleeps six in three bedrooms; Flat Two sleeps eight in three bedrooms (all beds supplied with duvets). Both flats are fully equipped, simply furnished, with colour TV. Bed linen and towels can be supplied at a charge. Open all year. Weekly terms from £100 to £225. Leaflet available from **Mr and Mrs Handley, Bragleenbeg, Loch Scammadale, Kilninver, By Oban PA34 4UU (08526 283).**

Self-catering Holidays in Unspoilt Argyll at
THE HIGHLAND ESTATE OF ELLARY AND CASTLE SWEEN

One of the most beautiful areas of Scotland with a wealth of historical associations such as St. Columba's Cave, probably one of the first places of Christian worship in Britain also Castle Sween, the oldest ruined castle in Scotland, and Kilmore Chapel where there is a fascinating collection of Celtic slabs.

PEACE, SECLUSION, OUTSTANDING SCENERY AND COMPLETE FREEDOM TO PURSUE INDIVIDUAL HOLIDAY PASTIMES. Loch, sea and burn fishing, swimming, sailing and observing a wide variety of wildlife can all be enjoyed on the estate and there are many signposted paths and tracks for the walker. Various small groups of cottages, traditional stone-built as well as modern, are strategically scattered throughout the estate. All have wonderful views and are near to attractive stretches of shore; in many cases there is safe anchorage for boats close by. Most of the cottages accommodate six, but one will take eight. All units are fully equipped except linen. TV reception is included in all but one cottage. For further details, brochure & booking forms please apply to:

ELLARY ESTATE OFFICE
By Lochgilphead, Argyll.
Ormsary (088-03) 232/209
or Achnamara (054 685) 223.

LOCHAWE. Innis Chonain, Loch Awe, Dalmally (083-82 220). Attractive three bedroom cottage on private 20 acre island (vehicle access by bridge from main A85 road). Superb situation on this beautiful loch with complete privacy, but only half a mile to shops. Ideal touring centre, Inveraray 17 miles, Oban 20 miles. Cottage has three bedrooms sleeping five/six persons. Modern furnishings, colour TV, electric heating, gas cooking, spin and tumble dryers. Linen not provided. Boat with free fishing on loch. Children welcome, pets permitted. Ample parking. Resident caretaker. Rates from £125 to £285 per week. Open all year. Full details from **J.C.D. Somerville, Ashton House, Pattingham Road, Perton, Wolverhampton WV6 7HD (0902 700644).**

See also Colour Display Advertisement **LOCHGILHPHEAD. Barmolloch Cottages, Barmolloch Farm, Kilmichael Glen, Lochgilphead PA31 8RJ (054 681209).** Peacefully situated midway along the scenic Kilmichael Glen on a steading that was a way station during the Great Cattle Droves from the Highlands and Islands. Three cottages, each sleeping six, with colour TV, electric central heating, washing machine/tumble dryer, fridge/freezer, microwave and dishwasher. All linen provided. Boat with engine and fishing equipment available. Mountain bikes for hire. One small dog by arrangement. Ideal area for walking, cycling, fishing, riding and touring. No smoking in the cottages. For a brochure write (enclosing SAE) or phone.

LOCHGOILHEAD. 2 Drimsynie Court, Lochgoilhead. Sleeps 9. Lochside Cottage, situated 300 yards

from the loch and the River Goil, and half-a-mile from the village, with magnificent views. Well equipped accommodation for nine in one single, four double rooms (one with bunk beds), plus cot and high chair; sitting/diningroom; kitchen with cooker, fridge/freezer, washing machine and spin dryer; bathroom with toilet; fully equipped except linen. Children and pets welcome. Shops half-a-mile. Ideal area for family holiday with walking, boating and fishing; facilities nearby for pony trekking, golf, tennis, bowls, curling, swimming and sailing. Within easy reach of Loch Lomond, Glasgow and Western Highlands. Tourist Board registered. Terms and brochure on application with SAE to **Mrs A.M. Lee, 51 School Lane, Solihull, West Midlands B91 2QG (Birmingham [021] 705 0201).**

NORTH CONNEL. Mrs D.I. Henderson, Birkmoss, Achnacree Bay, North Connel PA37 1RE (Connel [0631-71] 379). Sleeps 3. A small, modern, open-plan cottage situated in the spacious garden of the owner's house on the shore of Loch Etive. The accommodation comprises entrance vestibule, lounge with dining/kitchen area, having patio window overlooking the loch. The double bedroom and bathroom lead off from the livingroom. The settee in the lounge converts to an extra double bed if required. Beautifully furnished. Colour TV. Suitable for two/three persons. The property is on the Bonawe Road, three miles from Connel Bridge, eight miles from Oban. Car parking. Weekly terms £105 to £140. Electricity by 50p meter. Sorry, no pets.

OBAN. Omar Chalet. Three bedrooms (one double, one single and one with bunk beds), bathroom, lounge

and kitchen. Centrally heated, warm and comfortable. Electricity and gas. Situated on croft with lovely views of sea and beach. Beautiful surroundings with wild flowers, birds, rabbits in the wood by the chalet. Oban is eight miles, departure point for sailings to the Isles — Iona and many more. Good base for touring and a lovely part of Scotland. Not far from Fort William and Ben Nevis; forest walks locally. Open all year. Terms £80 to £180 (gas and electricity extra). Also available, caravan which sleeps four adults and child. Two bedrooms, shower, washbasin and toilet. Colour TV. Terms from £60 to £140 (gas and elctricity extra). **Mrs Violet MacKellar, "Seaview", Keil Croft, Benderloch, Oban PA37 1QS (0631 72360).**

See also Colour Display Advertisement **OBAN. Lag-na-Keil Chalets, Lerags, Oban PA34 4SE (0631 62746). Up to** 🏆🏆🏆🏆 *Commended.* **Properties sleep 2/8.** Ideal centre for Highlands and Islands. Lag-na-Keil offers peace and quiet in Lerags Glen, three and a half miles south of Oban on a seven acre wooded site with scenic views. Fully equipped one, two or three bedroom bungalows or chalets accommodating two/eight people; colour TV; everything supplied except linen. Children and pets welcome. Free fishing, boat for hire. Launderette and public telephone on site. Off-season reductions for two person bookings. Personal supervision. Available Easter to October. Phone or write (including SAE) for brochure to **John and Fiona Turnbull.**

See also Colour Display Advertisement **OBAN. Lonan House, Taynuilt PA35 1HY (Taynuilt [086-62] 253).** 🏆🏆🏆🏆 *Commended.* Nine independent self-catering spacious flats in a Scottish mansion with extensive beautiful grounds in the magnificent mountain setting of the West Highlands. TAYNUILT one mile, OBAN 12 miles. The flats are comfortably furnished and equipped with electric heating in all rooms. Colour TV, initial food delivery service, linen hire, pay phone, one, two or three bedrooms etc. Excellent centre for touring, riding, fishing, boating, sea trips, walking and climbing. Good local facilities for eating out. Also a chalet standing on its own in the grounds (sleeps two persons). ASSC member. Write or phone for colour brochure. Prices from £105 to £370 including VAT, electricity extra. Open April to October.

ELERAIG HIGHLAND CHALETS

Fully equipped Scandinavian chalets on secluded Eleraig estate near Oban, Argyll

Seven fully equipped chalets are set in breathtaking scenery in a private glen 12 miles south of Oban, gateway to the Highlands and Islands. The chalets are widely spaced, and close to Loch Tralaig where there is free brown trout fishing and boating – or bring your own boat. Chalets sleep 4-7. Peace and tranquillity are features of the site, located within an 1,800-acre working sheep farm.

Children and pets are especially welcome. Cots and high chairs are available. Walkers' and bird-watchers' paradise. Pony-trekking, sailing, golf, diving, gliding, water ski-ing and other sports, pastimes and evening entertainment are available locally. Car parking by each chalet.

Open March-November, and by negotiation. From £175/week/chalet including electricity.

Colour brochure from
resident owners:
Gill and Andrew Stevens,
Innie, Kilninver, by Oban,
Argyll PA34 4UX.
Telephone: Kilmelford (085 22) 225.

OBAN. Mrs Gill Cadzow, Duachy Farm, Kilninver, Oban PA34 4QN (Kilninver [08526] 244). Working farm. Properties sleep 5. Delightfully situated overlooking Loch Seil, Duachy Farm is about 10 miles south of Oban — an area of great natural beauty. Three attached cottages, converted from former farm buildings, located on both sides of an attractive courtyard. Two have an open-plan living/diningroom with kitchen area; shower room with WC. Double bedroom with one single bedroom (the larger cottage has an extra double bedroom). The third cottage has one double bedroom and one bedroom with two single beds; bathroom; open-plan living/diningroom with kitchen area. Colour TV in each cottage, cot and camp bed available. All cottages fully equipped for three to five people, including linen. Lots of hill walking. There is a rowing boat on the Loch for the use of tenants. Small beach about one mile — safe for swimming. Children and pets welcome. Car essential, parking. Open all year from £180 to £220 per week (including fuel). Scottish Tourist Board registered.

OBAN. Mrs Jill MacKenzie, The Mains, Hill Street, Oban PA34 5DG (0631 63879). The Mains is one of the oldest houses in Oban and faces south overlooking one of the town's many churches. It is in easy reach of shops, railway station and ferry pier. The ground floor flat consists of one double bedded room, bathroom, sittingroom with colour TV and kitchen area. No washing machine or phone but launderette and phone boxes within walking distance. Please bring own sheets, pillow cases and towels. Duvet and blankets provided. £155 per week plus electricity. Map available for exact location.

See also Colour Display Advertisement **OBAN near. J. Inglis, Raera Farm, Kilninver, Near Oban (Kilninver [085-26] 271). Working farm, join in. Properties sleep 4/6/8.** Raera Farm is a 500-acre hill farm with cattle and sheep, nine miles south of Oban. The River Euchar runs through the estate and salmon/sea trout fishing can be arranged. The farmhouse, cottage, chalet and studio flat are one mile from main road, reached by a tarred farm road. Raera House was built in 1743 — half of it is available for letting. It is self-contained, sleeps four/eight, has three bedrooms, sittingroom, kitchen, two bathrooms, storage heating throughout, and open fire. The cottage sleeps four/six and has two bedrooms, sittingroom, kitchen, bathroom, open fire and storage heaters. Chalet sleeps two/four and has one twin bedroom, sittingroom/kitchen, bathroom. Studio sleeps two/four and has one twin bedroom, sittingroom, kitchen and bathroom; storage heaters. All units have colour TVs. Car essential. Shopping best in Oban. Terms include electricity and downies. Pets allowed. Open all year. Wonderful area for wild life and bird enthusiasts; also many beautiful walks. Weekly terms on request with SAE, please. Tourist Board registered.

ESCAPE TO ANOTHER WORLD

TO TIMBER BUNGALOWS
on
COLOGIN FARM

THREE MILES SOUTH
OF OBAN

ONE OF OUR LARGE TIMBER BUNGALOWS

Yet set in a peaceful secluded glen amongst the hills in wild and open countryside. You can have a real country holiday away from it all in a Cologin Bungalow.

Here you will find complete freedom – you can do something different each day, or nothing, just as you fancy. Use a dinghy (and fishing rods if you want them) on our own trout loch or on the sea loch. Ride on a bike. Join in an informal accordion evening or a ceilidh / dance with a

kilted Highland piper. The old farm and surrounding countryside abound in a variety of wildlife, from herons and hares, to roe deer and foxes, and there are ducks, hens, guinea fowl, guinea pigs, a donkey, rabbits and a market garden on the old farm itself. In our games room or country pub you can play table tennis, pool, darts, dominoes, etc. In our area within two or three miles there are excellent facilities for golf, diving, fishing, swimming, sauna, tennis, bowls, pony trekking, squash, sailing and walking. We serve home-made bar meals all day in our own country pub and there are many other good hotels and restaurants at which to enjoy dining out within two or three miles. Our site is ideal for children. Pets welcome.

OPEN ALL YEAR ROUND

*THE OLD BYRE ON COLOGIN FARM –
NOW A COUNTRY PUB SERVING OUR BUNGALOWS*

Every bungalow is centrally heated, double glazed and fully insulated. It has an electric radiant fire, an electric cooker (with oven and grill) and fridge. Living rooms, bath and shower rooms, double/twin bedrooms and kitchens are all fully equipped. Shop and launderette on site, babysitting available. Colour TV, all electricity (except that used for bedroom heating) and bed linen are included in rentals. No charge is made for cots, high chairs or pets. Details from:

**Mr Henry B. Woodman, Cologin Homes Ltd., Cologin, Lerags, By Oban, Argyll PA34 4SE.
Telephone: Oban [0631] 64501 any time.**

OBAN by. Mr Henry R. Woodman, Cologin Homes Ltd., Cologin, Lerags, By Oban PA34 4SE (Oban [0631] 64501 — anytime). ♛♛♛ *Commended.* **Working farm. Bungalows sleep 2/6.** Open all year round — modern luxury timber bungalows on Cologin Farm, three miles south of Oban, yet set in peaceful private glen under the hills in wild and open countryside. Here you will find complete freedom — use of a dinghy (and fishing rods) on our own stocked trout loch or sea loch; ride on a bike; join in informal accordion evening or a ceilidh/dance with a kilted Highland piper. Every bungalow is centrally heated, double glazed, has electric heater, cooker, fridge (electricity included in rentals). Livingroom, bathroom, double/twin bedrooms all fully equipped; colour TV in all bungalows. Shop and launderette on site; babysitting available, also cots and high chairs. Linen included in rental. Site is ideal for children. Pets welcome. Country pub (table tennis, darts, dominoes etc.). SAE, please, for details. **See also Inside Front Cover of this guide.**

OBAN by. Mrs H.M. McCorkindale, Scammadale Farm, Kilninver, By Oban PA34 4UU (Kilninver [085-26] 282). **Working farm, join in. Sleeps 7.** Wing of old Scottish farmhouse of character, with own entrance, it stands in a beautiful position overlooking Loch Scammadale, 13 miles from Oban which has a lively night life and is the starting point for boat trips to the islands. Fishing in loch and river free to residents — includes boat. Furnishings simple and comfortable. Sleeps seven in one family bedroom, one twin-bedded room and a small single bedroom; bathroom/toilet; sitting/diningroom; colour TV. Kitchen has gas cooker and fridge etc. Guests must supply own linen. Sorry, no pets. Shops 13 miles away; sea five miles. Car essential — parking. Garage available. Terms from £110 to £230 weekly, including gas, lights and hot water. Electric fire and TV metered. SAE, please.

OBAN by. Mr D.R. Kilpatrick, Kilninver, By Oban PA34 4UT (Kilninver [085-26] 272 before 8.30pm). ♛♛♛♛ *Commended.* Kilninver is eight miles from Oban with its golf, pool, restaurants, cinema, cruises etc. The owners live on the estate. Houses and cottages on the 1000-acre estate, details of which are on the OUTSIDE BACK COVER of this publication. Boats, rods, cots, colour TV, laundry, dryers, fridges, heaters, milk, newspapers and trout fishing on two lochs included in rent. The accommodation includes flat, houses and cottages to sleep from four people to some accommodating nine. All details on request.

OBAN by. Achnacroish Cottage, Balvicar, Seil, By Oban. Sleeps 3. A former stone croft cottage, Achnacroish has been skilfully converted to retain its original character. It is situated 16 miles south of Oban, near the sea, on a croft containing sheep. It sleeps three in a double bedroom and an open-plan living area. There are electric radiators, an open fire and well-equipped kitchen. The area offers abundant wildlife and excellent walking, touring, sailing and fishing opportunities. Nearby is the former slate quarrying village of Easdale. Mull and Iona can be visited on day trips. Price, up to £175 per week, includes bed linen and towels but not electricity. Available May to September. Local shop half-mile and restaurants two miles. Easy parking; car essential. Regret no dogs. Member ASSC. **Further details: Dr and Mrs W. Lindsay, 11 Coulsdon Court Road, Coulsdon, Surrey CR3 2LL (081-660 5217).**

OBAN AREA. A choice of 40 properties sleeping from 2 to 10 persons. This property (illustrated) is just one from our range of high quality, individual, privately owned, self catering holiday homes. These include flats, cottages and houses in outstanding town, coast and country locations in Oban and Argyll. All properties are fully equipped to a high standard and have been personally inspected by ourselves. Locations and sizes to suit all tastes available on weekly terms from Saturday to Saturday from £115 to £650. Please write or telephone for a copy of our free illustrated brochure. **Highland Hideaways, (Alexander Dawson Estate Agents), 5/7 Stafford Street, Oban, Argyll PA34 5NJ (0631 62056 or 63901; Fax: 0631 66778).**

●
AWARDED
FARM
HOLIDAY
GUIDE
DIPLOMA
●

👑👑👑
Approved

Be independent with a cottage and a boat on

SKIPNESS ESTATE

On this unspoiled, peaceful, West Highland estate with its own historic castle and mediaeval chapel there are traditional estate-workers' cottages available to let all year round. Each cottage is well-equipped, including television, dinghy (except in winter months) and open fires. Laundry facilities and games room alongside the Seafood Cabin at Skipness Castle. Properties sleep four to ten people. Children and pets welcome. All cottages have magnificent views and beautiful surrounding countryside and coastline. Rocky coasts and sandy bays make for safe swimming, with sea, river and loch fishing, walks, pony-trekking and golf all nearby. Stalking can be arranged in season. Nearby ferries to Arran, Gigha, Islay and Jura. Apply for rates and further details to:

Mrs James, Skipness Estate, By Tarbert, Argyll PA29 6XU. Tel: Skipness 08806-207.

PORT APPIN. Field Cottage, Ardtur, Appin. A spacious bungalow used by its owners as a holiday home. Superb position, well away from public roads, overlooking Loch Linnhe with glorious views to Stalker Castle, the island of Lismore and the hills of Morvern and Mull. Beach at the bottom of the field below the cottage provides lovely walks and fun for children and boating enthusiasts. Good touring centre, Glencoe, Oban and Fort William in easy reach. Well equipped with freezer, washing machine, colour TV. Sleeps up to six adults plus two children. Two bathrooms. Ring **Appin (063173 555: answerphone in working hours)** or write **Bob Shiels, Ardtur, Appin PA38 4DD** for full details.

PORT APPIN. The Cottage, Port Appin. Sleeps 7. Situated on small bay 50 yards from beach. Sheltered

position, completely on its own, five minutes from the village. Area offers hill-walking, pony trekking, boating, windsurfing, sea fishing. Ideal for children. Oban and Fort William are within easy reach. Accommodation: four bedrooms; diningroom; sittingroom, kitchen and bathroom. Sleeps seven. Fully equipped. Electric cooker, fridge/freezer, washing machine, colour TV. No linen. Heating by electricity and coal fires. Available March-September £210 to £260 weekly. For details send SAE to **Mrs A.V. Livingstone, Bachuil, Isle of Lismore, By Oban PA34 5UL (063-176 256).**

TAYNUILT. Hazelbank, Taynuilt. Hazelbank Cottage is pleasantly situated in the owner's garden. The

cottage has been refurbished recently and comfortably accommodates two adults. The village of Taynuilt is 12 miles east of Oban offering a wide variety of facilities without the bustle of a holiday town. There are several hotels offering a variety of menus. Taynuilt is central for many of the holiday attractions in Argyll. Regret no pets. Weekly terms £100 to £160 (electricity by meter, hot water no charge). Contact: **Mr D.M. Harrison c/o Glencreran Estate, Scottish Agricultural College, Glencruitten Road, Oban PA34 4DW (0631 63093).**

TAYNUILT. Mrs R. Campbell-Preston, Inverawe House, Taynuilt PA35 1HU (Taynuilt [08662] 446; Fax: [08662] 274). Cottages sleep 6. Inverawe House set at the foot of Cruachan amid beautiful parkland, overlooking the River Awe, is four miles from Taynuilt and 16 from Oban (two miles off main A85 Glasgow — Oban Road at Bridge of Awe). It is ideally situated for a family holiday with fishing, boating, riding, tennis and walking. Nearby are three well stocked lochs, with trout up to 10 lbs, and salmon and seatrout fishing on the River Awe. Taynuilt offers a grocer, butcher, three hotels and a PO, whilst Oban has golf, swimming, shopping and cruises to the Islands. We have two charming cottages adjoining the house, sleeping five to six people, and consisting of two/three double bedrooms and bathroom upstairs; kitchen/diningroom, lounge and hall downstairs. Each fully equipped except linen. Electric cooker, fridge, TV, heating. Dogs welcome. Terms approximately £85 to £275 per week.

TAYVALLICH. 5 Kintallen, Tayvallich, By Lochgilphead. Charming, well equipped, modern cottage overlooking picturesque harbour. Maximum of six people and infant accommodated. Three double rooms, one with bunk beds, cot provided. Attic games room with table tennis. Sorry, no pets. Walk the woods and hills. Picnic on the beach. Boating. Short car ride to walk along Crinan Canal, golf in Lochgilphead, pony trekking or day trip to Oban or Inveraray. Explore the headlands birdwatching and sample the local seafish at the renowned Tayvallich Inn (two minutes' walk). Terms £120 to £250 per week. For further details telephone **05467 618** or SAE **Jeanie Wright, C/o Cariel, Tayvallich, Lochgilphead PA31 8PR.**

AYRSHIRE

BALLANTRAE. Mrs Audrey Young, Balnowlart Farm, Ballantrae KA26 0LA (Ballantrae [046-583] 227). ♥♥♥ *Commended.* **Working farm. Properties sleep 4/6.** One luxury country-lodge and one cedar bungalow, both situated in lovely Stinchar Valley near old fishing village of Ballantrae, with shopping facilities, seafishing, tennis court, putting green, bowling, golf courses within easy reach. Beautiful scenery, places of historic interest, many unspoilt beaches, with rock formation said to be oldest in the world. Ideal spot for touring the "Burns' Country, Alloway", also panoramic views at Glen Trool in "Bonnie Galloway". Daily sailings from Stranraer and Cairnryan to Northern Ireland. Accommodation is for six and four respectively. Sitting/diningrooms have open fires (fuel included), three bedrooms, bathroom, fully equipped electric kitchen, immersers. Metered electricity. Telephone. Tastefully furnished throughout. Linen, if necessary, available at a small extra fee. Ample parking — car essential. Pets by arrangement. Available all year. SAE, please, for terms.

GIRVAN. Carlenrig, Poundland, Pinwherry, Girvan. ♥♥♥♥ *Highly Commended.* **Sleeps 6.** Carlenrig is a luxury holiday cottage in the hamlet of Poundland with beautiful views of River Stinchar and surrounding hills. Come and relax in unspoilt countryside. Excellent base for coast or hills. Enjoy many places of interest including Culzean Castle, Burns' country and Glentrool Forest Park. Fishing, golfing, pony trekking, hill walking nearby. Cottage furnished, decorated and carpeted to a high standard. Sleeping six plus baby. Three bedrooms; bathroom, toilet; lounge with colour TV; pine style diningroom; fitted kitchen with electric cooker, fridge, washing machine. Sun porch, attractive secluded shrub and flower garden. Payphone. Car essential — parking. Pets and children welcome. Available all year from £85 to £225. Electricity extra. Storage heaters. SAE, please, for details. **Mrs Anne Shankland, "Talberg", Burnfoot Farm, Colmonell, Girvan KA26 0SQ (Colmonell [046-588] 265 or 220).**

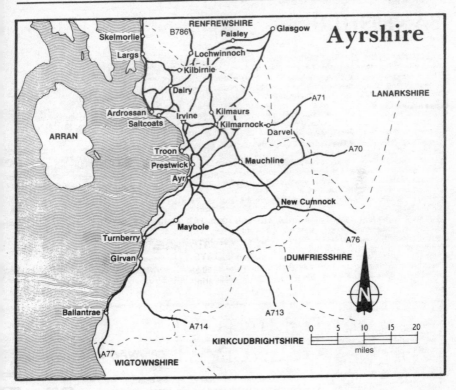

GIRVAN. Fairyknowe and Caldwell Cottages, Dowhill Farm, Turnberry, Girvan. Working farm.

Cottages sleep 6 adults plus cot. 🐝 🐝 🐝 *Approved.* Two semi-detached cottages 100 yards off the A77 coastal road, one and a half miles south of Turnberry on a 500 acre livestock farm. Each cottage is well equipped and comfortably furnished, cot and high chair available. Two bedrooms; kitchen with electric cooker, fridge, immersion heater, etc; bathroom; sittingroom, colour TV. Electric heaters. Electric blankets on all beds except bunk beds. Garden at rear of cottage and parking in front. Car not essential — shop within walking distance of properties, public transport 100 yards. Turnberry Championship Golf Course, Culzean Castle and Country Park nearby. Country road suitable for cyclists. Weekly terms from £120 excluding electricity. Bed linen provided. One pet only, by prior arrangement. Full particulars from **Miss M.Crawford, "Fairlight", Turnberry, Girvan KA26 9LW (0655 31331 or 31277).**

KILMARNOCK. Mrs Mary Howie, Hill House Farm, Grassyards Road, Kilmarnock KA3 6HG

(Kilmarnock [0563] 23370). Working farm. Sleep 6 and 9. Two properties within half a mile of each other situated on a working dairy farm in beautiful open countryside, two miles east of Kilmarnock. Easy access to Ayrshire coast and Burns country, sport and leisure centres. Excellent walking terrain and the cottages provide ideal base for touring or for the holidaymaker who enjoys golf, fishing or relaxing on sandy beaches. Fully equipped, very comfortable accommodation for six and nine people respectively comprising three or four bedrooms, cot, livingroom with colour TV, fire; kitchen with electric cooker, fridge, washing machine, etc. Storage heaters. Linen included. Weekly rates from £120 to £295. Tourist Board registered. Bed and Breakfast is available in the farmhouse from £12.

BANFFSHIRE

BALLINDALLOCH. Shenval, Ballindalloch, Glenlivet. Sleeps 9. The farmhouse is situated on the River Avon where fishing is available nearby, also near River Spey. Post Office, shop and filling station four miles. This is an ideal area for visiting whisky distilleries and for quiet country walks. Just 35 minutes' drive from Aviemore and 20 minutes' drive from Tomintoul. The farmhouse accommodates nine people in one double and two family bedrooms, cot; bathroom, toilet. Sittingroom has colour TV and Beta video. Diningroom. Kitchen has electric cooker, washing machine/tumble dryer and deep freeze. Open fire and gas heaters. No linen supplied. Children welcome. Pets permitted. Open from April to October and suitable for disabled guests. Terms from £120 weekly including fuel, 50p meter for electricity. Apply **Mrs M. Meldrum, Chapelton, Ballindalloch, Glenlivet AB9 3AL (Glenlivet [08073] 263).**

CARRON. Royne and Gardeners Cottages, Carron. Sleep 5/6. These attractive detached cottages are situated in the grounds of Laggan House, in a beautiful part of the Spey Valley. They are approached by private drive and are located near the Royne Burn some 200 yards from the River Spey. Carron Village is a short distance away and the shopping centre is in Aberlour, five miles from the cottages. Heating is by electric heaters, and there is an immersion heater for hot water. Bed linen and towels are provided. The cottages are within three-quarters of a mile of the Speyside Way, a popular choice with walkers. Prices from £110 to £200 weekly. For details contact: **Bidwells, Rothes Estate Office, Rothes, Aberlour AB38 7AD (03403 292).**

ROTHES. Kirkhill House, Near Rothes, Aberlour AB38 7AD (03403 292). Sleeps 8. Kirkhill House is a lovely old estate house which is situated in a beautiful part of the lower Spey Valley. It has a southerly aspect and is pleasantly isolated from neighbouring dwellings. The interior has been modernised and is carpeted throughout. There are four bedrooms with two single divan beds in each, a sizeable lounge comfortably furnished, and a good sized diningroom. The well fitted kitchen includes ample cupboard space. A deep freeze is provided. There is no cultivated garden, but ample grass area and good parking. Approximately three miles from Rothes for shopping. Weekly terms from £200 to £250.

BERWICKSHIRE

LONGFORMACUS. Dyeshaugh, Longformacus. ✦✦✦ *Commended.* **Sheep Farm. Sleeps 4/5.** Pretty stone-built cottage with large walled garden, garage and woodshed, peacefully situated by itself in the lovely Lammermuir Hills. Fishing in own waters, hill walking and wildlife to observe. Duns, 20 minutes away, has good shopping centre, golf and swimming with riding and trekking centre nearby. Well placed for visiting Edinburgh, Border Country and the lovely Berwickshire coast. Accommodation in two double and one single bedroom; all-electric kitchen with dining area, log fire in sittingroom; bathroom with heated towel rail and heater. Bed linen included. The cottage is prettily and very comfortably furnished throughout. Children and pets are welcome. Terms £195 per week including electricity and bed linen. **Mrs Sheila M. Pate, Horseupcleugh, Duns TD11 3PF (Longformacus [03617] 225).**

If you've found
FARM HOLIDAY GUIDES
of service please tell your friends

DUMFRIESSHIRE

CARLISLE. Mrs G. Elwen, Newpallyards, Hethersgill, Carlisle CA6 6HZ (0228 577 308). 🛇🛇🛇🛇 *Commended.* **GOLD AWARD WINNER.** Filmed for BBC TV. Relax and see beautiful North Cumbria and the Borders. A warm welcome awaits you on our 65-acre livestock farm tucked away in the Cumbrian countryside, yet easily accessible from M6 Junction 44. In addition to the surrounding attractions there is plenty to enjoy including nature walking, peaceful forests and sea trout/salmon fishing, ponies on the farm, or just nestle down and relax with nature. Self catering accommodation includes one comfortable well equipped bungalow with three/four bedrooms; two lovely cottages on a working farm with one/two bedrooms; and one well equipped flat with one bedroom. Terms from £80 to £295 weekly. AA, HWFB, FHB. Bed and Breakfast available at farmhouse.

EDINBURGH & THE LOTHIANS

THE ASSOCIATION OF SCOTLAND'S SELF CATERERS

CLEANLINESS, COMFORT COURTESY AND EFFICIENCY

ARE OUR IDEALS

The Association of Scotland's Self Caterers is an organisation of owners of holiday properties from cottages and chalets to flats, lodges and castles, who must prove they provide truly comfortable and pleasing accommodation before they are accepted for membership.

THEY CARE ABOUT YOU AND THE ENJOYMENT OF YOUR HOLIDAY. DON'T TAKE POT LUCK!

We have members throughout Scotland who offer high standards and good value for money – so you really don't have to. A free colour brochure will be sent by return by contacting A.S.S.C., 58 East Trinity Road, Edinburgh EH5 3EN Tel: 083-57-481.

EDINBURGH (18 miles). Mrs Geraldine Hamilton, Crosswoodhill Farm, West Calder EH55 8LP

(050185 205). ☙ ☙ ☙ *Commended.* **Sleeps 4 plus 2 in second livingroom.** Why not settle for the best of both worlds on this working farm? Rural seclusion, yet a half-hour drive takes you into historic Edinburgh, museums, palaces, galleries, theatres and fine shops. Glasgow 33 miles. Spectacular New Lanark 16 miles. Perfect base for touring the Borders, Trossachs and over the Forth to Fife and Perthshire. Boat trips, pony trekking, mountain biking less than an hour away. Even closer: golfing, fishing, hillwalking, exploring our 1700 acre livestock farm on the northern slopes of the Pentlands. Comfort, charm, warmth, tradition and a friendly welcome await you in a self contained wing of our spacious 200 year old farmhouse with your own garden. Full central heating. Well equipped including colour TV, electric cooker, washing machine, tumble dryer, fridge freezer, all bed linen and towels. Dogs by arrangement (sheep country). Extras: home-grown peat and coal for multi-fuel stove at cost; electricity by meter reading. Own transport essential. Layout: own entrance, kitchen, living/dining room. Upstairs: bathroom, three rooms sleep six (one double, one pair adult bunks, one double/one single in lounge). Cot available. Terms from £130 to £260 weekly. Telephone or SAE for brochure.

INVERNESS-SHIRE

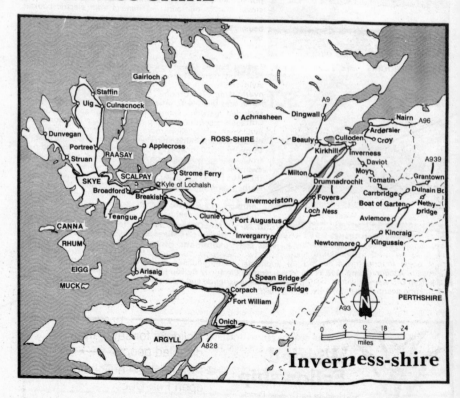

Inverness-shire

ARISAIG. Mr A.A. Gillies, Kinloid Farm, Arisaig PH39 4NS (068-75 366). ☙ ☙ Working farm. AA approved. Three new holiday cottages widely spaced on a naturally sloping site, each commanding magnificent views across Arisaig to the sea and the islands of Skye, Rhum and Eigg. Five minutes by car from wonderful sands. Ideal area for fishing, hill walking and golf. The cottages are modern, roomy and comfortable; well insulated and suitable for holidays at any time of the year. Comfortably furnished lounge with colour TV; two bedrooms; bathroom with shower; fully fitted kitchen with electric cooker and fridge. Electricity for heating and lighting. Sorry, no pets. Terms from £150 per week. SAE, please, for brochure. Huge reductions early and late season.

ARISAIG. A. and B. Moynihan, Self Catering Holidays, Arisaig PH39 4NS (06875 667). Cottage and Chalets newly built on a Highland croft at Arisaig. View of the Isles of Skye, Rhum and Eigg. Each unit is fully furnished and equipped to a high standard including fridge, washing machine, colour TV. Within easy reach of shops, hotel and seashore. Steam train runs daily in Summer. Well behaved pets welcome. Phone or write for details.

CARRBRIDGE by. Liz and Ian Bishop, Slochd Cottages, By Carrbridge PH23 3AY (Carrbridge [047984] 666; Fax: 047984 699). Cottages sleep 6. A row of three cottages, set in their own grounds, off the new A9, four miles north of Carrbridge. Ideally placed for touring and convenient for Aviemore and the Cairngorms. Inverness and Loch Ness 20 miles. Cross-country ski and mountain bike hire and wonderful forest and mountain trails from the doorstep. Ski-ing, sailing, windsurfing, canoeing, golfing, fishing, pony trekking etc within easy reach. Each cottage has porch, dining/sittingroom; central heating and wood burning stove; double bedroom; kitchenette with electric cooker; shower and separate WC; upstairs bedroom with four single beds. Fully equipped including linen. Cot available. Well behaved pets welcome. Open all year. Terms from £115. Fuel extra. Weekend and short stays by arrangement. SAE for further details please.

DRUMNADROCHIT. Mrs J.L.M. Younie, Garbeg Farm, Drumnadrochit IV3 6XS (045-62 331). Working farm. Sleeps 6. Attractive traditional Highland-style cottage situated high on the hills of Garbeg Farm, overlooking Glen Urquhart with breathtaking views of Glen Affric and the Western Mountains. Surrounded by its own secluded garden, with ample parking space, "Garbeg Cottage" accommodates up to six in three bedrooms (cot available); sitting/diningroom; fully equipped kitchen with electric cooker, fridge, spin dryer; bathroom. Electric heating throughout (50p meter). Local holiday pursuits include free trout fishing, walking, pony trekking, golf, tennis, bowls, swimming in lochs. In Drumnadrochit, three miles away, there is a choice of hotels, garages, shops, bank and a doctor. Garbeg is in the centre of open countryside — perfect for exploring, finding rare birds and plants. Scottish Countryside Commission award for Conservation and Best Farm Woodlands in Scotland 1987. Weekly terms from £90 to £250. SAE please for brochure and further details.

See also Colour Display Advertisement **FOYERS. Mr i.J. MacDougall, Patmac Holiday Enterprises, 103 Church Street, Inverness IV1 1ES (0463 713702). Properties sleep 5/6.** Holiday cottages situated in the village of Foyers, Loch Ness-side, 19 miles south of Inverness. Each property accommodates five/six guests. All are modernised and furnished with two bedrooms, one double and the other with double and single beds; lounge has sofa bed for additional accommodation. TV. Shower room with toilet and handbasin. Kitchen/dining area with cooker, fridge. Electricity by 50p slot meter. Linen/towels on request. Rates from £45 weekly, winter. SAE please for full description and colour brochure. We can also offer some self-catering accommodation in Inverness itself.

S.T.B. COMMENDED

GLEN NEVIS HOLIDAY COTTAGES

Modern, purpose-built cottages in the midst of the best of Highland scenery in famous Glen Nevis, close to mighty Ben Nevis. Enjoy peaceful surroundings, with lots to see and do nearby. Our own spacious restaurant and lounge bar is only a short walk away and the historic town of Fort William only 2½ miles distant. Well equipped, insulated and heated, colour television, laundry facility etc. Ideal for holidays at any time of the year.
Brochure: Glen Nevis Holiday Cottages, Glen Nevis, Fort William, Inverness-shire. PH33 6SX.
Tel: (0397) 702191. B4

INVERGARRY. Miss J. Ellice, Taigh-an-Lianach, Aberchalder Farm, Invergarry PH35 4HN (08093 287). Three self-catering properties, all ideal for hill walkers and country lovers. Salmon and trout fishing available. ABERCHALDER LODGE, traditional Highland shooting lodge, extensively modernised to give high standard of comfort, sleeps 12. TAIGH-AN-LIANACH, modern self-contained bed-sit, secluded and peaceful, sleeps two. LEAC COTTAGE, a secluded cottage which combines old world charm with a high standard of comfort, sleeps three. Regret, no pets. Fort William Tourist Board registered.

INVERNESS. Mr and Mrs R.M. Pottie, Easter Dalziel Farm, Dalcross, By Inverness IV1 2JL (0667 462213). From ♛♛♛ Commended to ♛♛♛ Highly Commended. Sleep 4/6 adults. Our three traditional stonebuilt Cottages, all fully equipped to a high standard including linen, are situated midway between Inverness and Nairn on our stock/arable farm. Each property has colour TV, fridge, cooker, washing machine. The surrounding rich habitat is a haven for wildlife. Sometimes pet lambs and chicks to feed. Local attractions include Cawdor Castle, Culloden, Fort George and Loch Ness. Aviemore 30 miles. Central for scenic day trips, e.g. Deeside, Ullapool and John O'Groats. Sporting facilities at Inverness and Nairn. Open all year. Short off season breaks available. Telephone for brochure.

Key to Tourist Board Ratings

The Crown Scheme
(England, Scotland & Wales)

Covering hotels, motels, private hotels, guesthouses, inns, bed & breakfast, farmhouses. Every Crown classified place to stay is inspected annually. *The classification:* Listed then 1-5 Crown indicates the range of facilities and services. Higher quality standards are indicated by the terms APPROVED, COMMENDED, HIGHLY COMMENDED and DELUXE.

The Key Scheme
(also operates in Scotland using a Crown symbol)

Covering self-catering in cottages, bungalows, flats, houseboats, houses, chalets, etc. Every Key classified holiday home is inspected annually. *The classification:* 1-5 Key indicates the range of facilities and equipment. Higher quality standards are indicated by the terms APPROVED, COMMENDED, HIGHLY COMMENDED and DELUXE.

The Q Scheme
(England, Scotland & Wales)

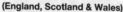

Covering holiday, caravan, chalet and camping parks. Every Q rated park is inspected annually for its quality standards. The more √ in the Q – up to 5 – the higher the standard of what is provided.

INVERNESS by. Lentran Farm Holiday Cottages, By Inverness. 👑👑 *Commended.* **Working farm. Cottages sleep 4/6.** A selection of three comfortable holiday cottages situated about half a mile from the main road at Lentran Home Farm. Each cottage is fully furnished including cutlery and bedding, but linen and towels not provided, though they can be hired. Each is equipped with electric cooker, immersion heater, electric fire, fridge, electric kettle, iron and shaver points. Colour TV. Metered electricity. Babies' cots available. Overlooking the Beauly Firth, this is an ideal position for touring. Ullapool two hours away. Nairn, Findhorn and Lossiemouth even closer. Inverness six miles. Well behaved dogs allowed. Available May to October. Weekly terms from approximately £85 to £230. Details from: **Mrs S. Lawson, The Stackyard, Pitglassie Farm, Dingwall, Ross-shire IV15 9TR (Dingwall [0349] 62249 or 62004).**

See also Colour Display Advertisement **INVERNESS. Mr F.S. Matheson, Na Tighean Beaga, East Park, Roy Bridge PH31 4AG (Spean Bridge [039-781] 370/436).** A small private development of bungalows and chalets. Fort William 12 miles, close to Rivers Spean and Roy with splendid views over Glen Spean and Ben Nevis mountain range. Ideal for climbing, walking, fishing. The units are well appointed and furnished, with bed linen supplied but not towels. Quality homes for two/eight persons, each is self-contained, all-electric, fully carpeted, colour TV, two/four bedrooms, sittingroom, dinette with cooker, fridge, modern units. Bathrooms have bath or shower, some both. Heating all rooms. Laundry with washing machine, etc. Metered electricity. Shop 300 yards. Parking. Pets welcome. **Member of BH&HPA and ASSC. Weekly terms £125 to £440 (including VAT). Short Breaks from £60 for two days** SAE for further details.

See also Colour Display Advertisement **KIRKHILL (near Inverness). Mr M.R. Fraser, Reelig House, Reelig Glen, Kirkhill, Near Inverness IV5 7PR (046-383 208).** 👑👑 *Approved to* 👑👑👑 *Commended.* **Properties sleep 4/5.** Holiday cottages and chalets in secluded woodland positions only eight miles from Inverness, capital of the Highlands. People staying here have enjoyed the freedom and the solitude; the tall trees and water of the Fairy Glen; the countryside with all the untrammelled joys of nature is at the door, butterflies find what butterflies need. Yet they have been glad of the nearness to shops, the pleasures of Inverness and of Beauly only 10 minutes' drive away. Pony trekking, sandy beaches and organised pastimes not far off. Central for touring West Coast to North, Central Highlands, Glen Affric, Culloden, Aviemore, Speyside and Moray Firth coast. The holiday homes sleep from four to five people and are fully equipped except for linen and towels (unless these are specially asked for), with electric fires, night storage heater, fridge, shaving socket and colour TV. Reduced rates spring and autumn. Brochure available.

ROYBRIDGE. Mrs Christine MacDonald, Tulloch Farm, Roybridge PH31 4AR (039 785 217; Fax: 039 785 309). 👑👑👑 We have two holiday cottages, one flat and a bothy sleeping from two to five persons. They are six miles from the village of Roybridge and ideally situated for enjoying a West Highland holiday of tranquil pleasure — be it fishing, ski-ing, walking, clay pigeon shooting or just taking it easy. You will be in your element here. Properties are fully equipped throughout. Cooking and heating by gas. Bed linen supplied. Car essential, ample parking. Terms from £180 to £280 weekly. Bed and Breakfast also available. Brochure.

See also Colour Display Advertisement **STRONTIAN. Hamish Howland, Seaview Grazings, Strontian PH36 4HZ (0397 702496).** 👑👑👑 *Highly Commended.* Why not fall under the spell of our Highland Magic? Relax in a log cabin amidst majestic mountains overlooking the sparkling waters of Loch Sunart. Each cabin has central heating, colour TV, fridge/freezer, automatic washing machine, free linen and electricity. The area is ideal for exploring, walking, bird watching, messing about in boats, fishing, hill walking or just enjoying peace and quiet. Terms from £200 to £450.

KIRKCUDBRIGHTSHIRE

CASTLE DOUGLAS. Mr H.G. Ball, Barncrosh, Castle Douglas DG7 1TX (Bridge of Dee [055-668] 216; Fax: [055-668] 442). 👑👑👑 *Commended.* **Properties sleep 2/4/6/8.** BARNCROSH FARM, our home, nestles amid rolling Galloway countryside. Visitors are welcome to wander in the fields and woods. All the accommodation is of a high standard (up to four crowns commended), centrally heated, fully equipped, with all linen supplied and colour TV. The OLD FARMHOUSE sleeps six in three double bedrooms, one with a double bed, one room with twin beds and one with full sized bunk beds. Ground floor has a spacious kitchen/diningroom adjoining a utility room with washing machine. There is also a large lounge with electric heating. A downstairs cloakroom supplements the upstairs bathroom. KILTARLILTIE, a former gamekeeper's cottage (Grade III listed) has been fully modernised and sleeps four in two bedrooms, one with double bed and the other with full size bunk beds. Lounge, kitchen, toilet and shower complete the accommodation. The FLATS have been converted from the old stone-built stable block and are self-contained with individual access. Accommodation is of a high standard for two/four people. GALLOWAY has something special to offer all the family. From £95 to £350 weekly. Please do not hesitate to write or phone for further details. A warm welcome is assured to all our guests.

CASTLE DOUGLAS. Cala-Sona, Auchencairn, Castle Douglas. Sleeps 6. A stone-built house in centre of Auchencairn village, near shops, post office and garage. To let, furnished. Equipped for six persons. Linen not supplied. Two bedrooms (one double bed; two single beds); cot available. Bathroom, sittingroom with bed settee, livingroom and kitchenette with electric cooker, fridge and geyser. Auchencairn is a friendly seaside village and you can enjoy a peaceful holiday here on the Solway Firth where the Galloway Hills slope down to the sea. Many places of historic interest to visit, also cliffs, caves and sandy beaches. A haven for ornithologists. SAE brings prompt reply. Car essential — parking. **Mrs Mary Gordon, 7 Church Road, Auchencairn, Castle Douglas DG7 1QS (Auchencairn [055-664] 345).**

CASTLE DOUGLAS by. Mrs S. Ward, Auchenshore, Auchencairn, By Castle Douglas DG7 1QZ

(Auchencairn [055-664] 244). ✿✿ Commended. Properties sleep 2/5/6. The property, situated by Balcary Bay, consists of three cottages, within 100 yards of the sea, in beautiful countryside. Ideal area for walking, bird watching, fishing, windsurfing and other sporting activities, including golf and riding. Dundrennan Abbey and Thrieve Gardens (National Trust) nearby. Courtyard Cottage accommodates five in two double and one single room; Long Cottage takes six in three double rooms and the Studio can accommodate two in one room. Properties are well heated, comfortably furnished and fully equipped. Two cottages are suitable for the disabled. Shops two miles — car essential. Pets welcome. Play area. Tourist Board registered. Weekly from £70 to £225. Colour brochure on application.

DUMFRIES. Mrs J.P.R. Deans, Ingleston Farm, New Abbey, Dumfries DG2 8DG (New Abbey [038-785] 204). Cottage sleeps 7. Farm cottage with garden in secluded position overlooking the Solway, has three bedrooms, plus cot. Bathroom with heated towel rail and electric shower; sitting/diningroom with colour TV and electric or coal fire; kitchen with electric cooker, fridge, immersion heater, washing machine, spin dryer, pulley and electric iron. Night store heaters and electric blankets are supplied. Pets permitted. Weekly terms on request. SAE, please.

GALLOWAY. "Blairmac", 6 Main Street, Auchencairn, Castle Douglas. The house is detached with garden and garage. "Blairmac" accommodates six in three double bedrooms plus cot. Diningroom, sittingroom, kitchen, bathroom with shower and shaving point. Electric fires. Linen supplied. TV. Children welcome, pets permitted. Open all year. Auchencairn is an ideal base for touring south-west Scotland — beaches, golf courses, bowling greens, historic buildings all within easy driving distance. Lots of Local walks. Terms from £110 to £150 per week. Contact **Mrs Lilian Wilson, 33 Main Street, Auchencairn, Castle Douglas DG7 1QU (055-664 285).**

ROCKCLIFFE. Kirkland Farmhouse, Rockcliffe. ✿✿✿✿ Commended. Very attractive granite farm-

house, newly modernised to a high standard, with pine furniture, fitted carpets, plenty of heating. Delightful large secluded garden. One mile Rockcliffe Beach. GROUND FLOOR: lounge with colour TV; fitted kitchen; pantry with fridge/freezer; washing machine, spin dryer. Diningroom, double bedroom, shower/WC. UPSTAIRS: four double bedrooms (one double bed); bathroom and WC, heated towel rails. Washbasins in bedrooms. Cot, high chair. Surrounded by owners' farm and fields up a private drive. Lovely moorland and seaside walks; pony trekking, golf nearby. Sailing. Free coarse fishing. Fully equipped for eight persons plus a baby. Terms from £115. Special rates for four or less in off-peak season. SAE for terms **Mrs S. Sinclair, Mount of Glenluffin, Rockcliffe, Dalbeattie DG5 4QG (055663 205).**

LANARKSHIRE

BIGGAR. Carmichael Country Cottages, Carmichael Estate Office, Westmains, Carmichael, Biggar ML12 6PG (08993 336; Fax: 08993 481). 🏆🏆🏆/🏆🏆🏆🏆 *Commended.* **Working farm, join in. Sleep 2/9.** These 200-year-old stone cottages nestle among the woods and fields of our 700-year-old family estate. Still managed by the descendants of the original Chief of Carmichael. We guarantee comfort, warmth and a friendly welcome in an accessible, unique, rural and historic time capsule. We farm deer, cattle and sheep and sell meats and tartan — Carmichael of course! Children and pets welcome. Open all year. Terms from £160 to £395. FHB Member. ASSC member. 12 cottages with a total of 25 bedrooms. We have the ideal cottage for you. Private tennis court and fishing loch; cafe and farm shop.

GLASGOW. Mrs C. Chambers, 195 Wilton Street, Glasgow G20 (041-946 1724). Sleep 2/4. Two self catering flats situated just 10 minutes from City Centre available from January to December. Weekly rates from £170 to £280 (gas and electricity extra). Minimum letting period weekend. Flats are comprehensively furnished with all usual amenities; kitchen equipment; shower; iron; provision for child. Terms from £170 to £280 weekly. Further details available on request.

MORAYSHIRE

BALLINDALLOCH. Glenarder, Ballindalloch. Sleeps 8. Glenarder is situated about one mile off the B9102 road in the heart of Speyside. It is equidistant from coastal areas and the Cairngorms, both providing a much varied contrast in entertainment. It is a peaceful area and gives freedom to children and pets. The nearest shops and petrol station five miles away. Accommodation comprises three bedrooms (two large, one small), scullery, pantry, kitchen/diningroom and sittingroom. Fridge, electric cooker, washing machine etc. are all supplied. Oil-fired Rayburn ensures constant hot water. No linen supplied. Car essential — parking. Off season £120 per week — peak period £180. Send SAE to **Mrs Anne M. Dean, Kirdellbeg, Ballindalloch, Banffshire AB3 9BS (Ballindalloch [080-72] 233).**

PEEBLESSHIRE

PEEBLES. Mrs C. Campbell, Glenrath Farm, Kirkton Manor, Peebles EH45 9JW (072 740 221 or 226). 🏆🏆🏆/🏆🏆🏆🏆🏆 *Commended.* **Sleep 6/8.** We have two luxury farmhouses and five cottages situated in three separate locations, all within 15 minutes of the town of Peebles, and one farmhouse cottage 25 minutes from Edinburgh. The farms are all working hill sheep farms and cover approximately 5000 acres. We have excellent hill walking, coarse and river fishing (free) on a tributary of the River Tweed which runs through the farm for four miles. Permits available for salmon fishing in Peebles. Mountain biking, excellent golf courses, swimming, tennis, horse riding and plenty of good restaurants in Peebles. Very suitable for children. Pets also welcome. The properties are graded from three to five crowns by the STB and all except one has three bedrooms. Colour TV, telephone, washing machine, white meter storage heating, fridges. All cottages have open fires. Linen available. We also have two one-bedroomed flats in Peebles two minutes from High Street, sleeps three; three crowns STB. Bed and Breakfast also available except July and August. Member Farm Holiday Bureau and ASSC.

See also Colour Display Advertisement **WEST LINTON. Mrs C.M. Kilpatrick, Slipperfield House, West Linton EH46 7AA (West Linton [0968 60401].** 🏆🏆🏆/🏆🏆🏆🏆 *Commended.* **Cottages sleep 4/6.** Two Commended cottages a mile from West Linton at foot of Pentland Hills, set in 100 acres of lochs and woodlands. **America Cottage** sleeps six in three bedrooms, is secluded and has recently been modernised. Equipment includes washing machine, dryer, microwave oven and telephone. **Loch Cottage** sleeps four in two bedrooms and is attached to owner's house; magnificent views over a seven acre loch. Both cottages have sittingroom with dining area and colour TV; modern bathrooms; excellently equipped Schreiber kitchens. Controlled pets allowed. Car essential — ample parking. Golf and private fishing. Edinburgh 19 miles. Available all year. SAE for terms.

PERTHSHIRE

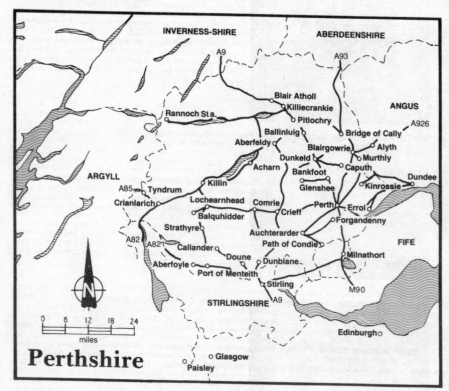

Perthshire

ABERFELDY. Mrs E. Duncan Millar, Remony, Acharn, Aberfeldy PH15 2HR (0887830 209).

♛♛♛♛ *Highly Commended.* **Properties sleep 2/4/6/8.** These traditional agricultural workers' cottages have been totally modernised and are suitable for summer and winter use, having open fires, radiators, colour TV, fridge, washing machine and a tumble dryer in the drying rooms. Linen and towels are provided. They are on the edge of the picturesque farming village of Acharn with parking outside and private ground down to the loch with special facilities for fishing and sailing. Ideal for bird watching and walking with several golf courses within an hour's drive including Gleneagles. Children and dogs welcome. Cots etc available. Terms £140 to £375 per week. Colour brochure.

ABERFELDY. Lyon Bank Cottage, Croftgarrow Farm, Fortingall, Aberfeldy. Working farm, join in. Cottage sleeps 4. Quaint farm cottage, very well equipped, extremely cosy, recently decorated throughout. Two bedrooms, one double and one twin-bedded, cot; bathroom, toilet; sittingroom, old beamed dining-room. Electric cooker. Fully fitted carpets throughout. Pets welcome. Car essential; ample parking. One mile to shops. All outdoor activities catered for including golf, walking, pony trekking, watersports on nearby Loch Tay. Trout fishing rights with cottage on River Lyon. Garden at front, lawn at rear. All year bookings; terms range from £90 to £140 weekly according to season. Also out of season weekends and breaks at special rates. Guests must supply own bedlinen. Further details from **Mrs G. McGregor, Balnald, Fortingall, Aberfeldy PH15 2LL (0887 830384).**

ABERFELDY. Tynayare, Fortingall, Aberfeldy. ♛ **Sleeps 5.** From May to October a peaceful, small farmhouse with good access road and beautiful views of Glen Lyon is available for holiday letting. Situated close to River Lyon, with pony trekking, golf and sailing about two miles away. Accommodation for five persons in two double, one single bedrooms; bathroom, two toilets; livingroom; fully equipped kitchen, electric cooker, fridge etc. Everything supplied except linen. Electrically heated, the house is suitable for disabled visitors. Car essential, parking. Shops two miles. Children and pets welcome. Good touring centre — places of interest include Pitlochry, Aviemore, Oban, Edinburgh — all within easy distance. Terms from £100 to £150 per week. SAE, please, for terms. **Mrs J.M. Kininmonth, Kinnighallen, Fortingall, Aberfeldy PH15 2LR (0887 830 327).**

ABERFELDY. Mrs J.M. McDiarmid, Mains of Murthly, Aberfeldy PH15 2EA (0887 820427). 🐾🐾🐾

Cottages sleep 4/6. Two beautifully situated holiday cottages overlooking Aberfeldy on a working farm, one and a quarter miles from shops. Pony trekking, tennis, fishing, shooting and golf available nearby. New recreation centre and swimming pool in Aberfeldy. Fully equipped for four/six persons. Dining/sittingroom, kitchen, bathroom. Everything supplied except linen. Hire service available. Children welcome, cot provided. Pets acceptable. Ample parking. Available all year, with terms from £110. SAE, please, for further details.

ALYTH. Kerry Cottage, East Tullyfergus Farm, Alyth. Sleeps 4/6. Secluded position on working stock and arable farm situated two miles from Alyth, four miles Blairgowrie. Within easy reach of places of historic interest, fishing, golf, walking and Glen Shee ski slopes. Visitors may help on the farm if they wish. Pleasant garden and ample parking. Fitted kitchen with electric cooker and fridge-freezer.

Bathroom. Living room — logs provided for an open fire which will heat water and radiators. Immersion heater. Electric fire (50p meter) and Dimplex radiators also available. First bedroom has twin beds, second bedroom is a large room with double bed and bunks. Cot also available. Linen and duvets provided for beds. Sleeping bags required for bunks and linen for cot. Charges from £100 per week. Apply to **Mrs J.A. Groom, East Tullyfergus Farm, Alyth PH11 8JY (082-83 3251).**

BLAIRGOWRIE. Ardblair Castle, Blairgowrie PH10 6SA (0250 873155). 🐾🐾🐾🐾 *Highly Commended.* **Properties sleep 5/11.** Open all year. Ski-ing, fishing, golfing, touring. Delightful 19th century stable set in picturesque castle grounds. COACH HOUSE comprises one double and one treble-bedded rooms with washbasin. All facilities on ground level. THE STABLE comprises twin bunkroom, one twin and one treble-bedded room with washbasin, two bathrooms. Built in 1780 THE FARMHOUSE, traditionally furnished, sleeps 11. Three double, two twin, one single-bedded rooms. Bathroom and utility/shower room. All houses have fully fitted kitchens, colour TV, automatic washing machines and payphones. Linen is provided.

Electricity metered. Sorry, no pets. Brochure and terms on request: **J. Blair Oliphant, Ardblair Castle, Blairgowrie PH10 6SA (0250 873155).**

BLAIRGOWRIE. Mrs K.A.L. Saddler, Inverquiech, Alyth, Blairgowrie PH11 8JR (Alyth [08283] 2463). Working farm. Cottage sleeps 4. Open all year — this stone-built cosy cottage with garage attached is situated in attractive agricultural surroundings beside the River Isla. Well furnished sitting-cum-diningroom with colour TV and open fire. Off-peak central heating. Two twin-bedded rooms, electric blankets and linen supplied. Fitted kitchen with all amenities; bathroom. Controlled pets welcome. Facilities nearby for riding, golfing, fishing, walking, swimming, theatres, ski-ing etc. Small private garden. Cottage lies adjacent to, but separate from, farmhouse. Terms: £100 to £140. Electricity and coal extra, logs free. Special rates off-season short breaks. SAE please.

BLAIRGOWRIE near. Mrs E. D. Church, Easter Drimmie, Bridge of Cally, Near Blairgowrie PH10 7JD (Bridge of Cally [025-086] 359). Cottages sleep 5/6.

Two adjoining cottages, fully furnished and equipped, linen extra, peacefully situated a few miles north of Blairgowrie amidst splendid countryside on upland farm. **Mill Cottage** has two double, one bunk-bedded rooms (sleeps six). Sittingroom; bathroom/toilet; well-equipped kitchen with dining area. **Stable Cottage** is attractively timbered inside. Sleeps five/six in one large family bedroom (double and single beds), one twin bedroom with wash-hand basin. One large living/diningroom. Well equipped kitchen. Bathroom/toilet. Cots available. Car essential — parking. Controlled pets permitted. Ideal hill walking/touring. Pitlochry, Perth, Braemar, Edinburgh within easy reach. Golf, tennis court, riding, fishing, water ski-ing, wildfowl sanctuary and many historically interesting places nearby. Weekly terms from £110. SAE, please, for details.

COMRIE. Lady Jauncey, Tullichettle, Comrie (Comrie [0764] 70349). Sleeps 4. The Bothy is an unusual 18th-century cottage converted from a stable into a modernised, comfortable holiday home. Peaceful location with magnificent views of the Aberuchill Hills, which lie across fields beyond the River Ruchill. Fishing available in River Earn, River Ruchill and Loch Earn. Many interesting and scenic walks. Good golf course in village; bowling 10-minute walk. Accommodation in two twin-bedded rooms, bathroom, sitting/diningroom. Kitchen with all electrical equipment, cooker, fridge, dishwasher, kettle, spin dryer. Everything except linen supplied. Shops one mile. Car advisable — parking. Garden area. Dogs only by prior arrangement. Available March to end October. Terms from £170 to £240. Further details on request.

CRIANLARICH. "Cottages," Inverchaggernie, Crianlarich. Cottages sleep 6. Two cedarwood cottages, situated beside the Inverchaggernie Burn in a sheltered position on a hill farm, one and a half miles west of Crianlarich on Oban road; train services (West Highland Line), grocers store, hotel, church, 'phone etc. This is an excellent touring centre and many interesting places can be visited in a short time — Oban, where boats can be hired to Mull, Iona etc., Inveraray Castle, Killin, with the famous Falls of Dochart, Loch Lomond and the Safari Park at Blair Drummond. Fishing in river and loch included in price. Hill walking — the West Highland Way passes through the Glen. Canoe hire and instruction available. Both cottages accommodate six in two bedrooms (one bunks, one double), bed-settee in combined sitting/diningroom; bathroom, toilet; kitchen with electric cooker, fridge, kettle, immersion heater. Linen may be supplied. Well controlled pets allowed. Available from March to November. Weekly terms from £95. Car essential, parking. SAE to **Mrs C.S.R. Christie, Lochdochart, Crianlarich FK20 8QS (Crianlarich [083-83] 274).**

CRIANLARICH. North Wing, Lochdochart House, Crianlarich. Sleeps 9. Wing of large mansion house

to let fully furnished. Situated in mature policy grounds adjacent to loch and river. Access by half mile tarred private road. Four miles east of Crianlarich on A85. Upstairs: three bedrooms (two double, third has three single beds); bathroom with over-bath shower. Stair not suitable for disabled guests. Livingroom with open coal fire (coal provided), colour TV and couch which makes into double bed. Fully equipped large modern kitchen/diningroom with fridge/freezer, electric cooker (auto oven timer), dishwasher, automatic washing machine. Bed linen can be hired. Grocers in village, also post office, church, phone box, two licensed restaurants, railway station on the West Highland Line. Excellent touring centre — Oban (about an hour) with boats to Mull, Iona etc. Many picturesque and interesting places to visit. Free fishing to tenants, hill walking on West Highland Way. Canoe hire and instruction available. Sorry, no dogs. Open all year, from £150 per week. **Mrs C.S.R. Christie, Lochdochart, Crianlarich FK20 8QS (Crianlarich [083-83] 274).**

DUNKELD by. Mrs M.H. Bruges, Laighwood, Butterstone, By Dunkeld PH8 0HB (0350 724241).

🟣🟣🟣 *Commended.* **Properties sleep 3/5.** Two cottages and two flats on a large sheep farm, with private trout fishing and squash court. Available from April to October. The cottages, with beautiful views, stand by themselves up private tarmac roads. The flats adjoin Butterglen House beside Butterstone Loch. All are carpeted throughout, have bathroom and WC, and are fully equipped including electric cooker, fridge, immersion heater, electric blankets and colour TV. Cot and high chair available. Linen for hire. Three have open fires. Electric slot meters. Car essential. Butterstone lies in magnificent countryside (especially Spring/Autumn), adjacent to Nature Reserve (ospreys). Central for walking, sporting facilities, touring, historic houses. Sorry, no pets. Terms from £83 to £185 weekly. SAE, please.

Terms quoted in this publication may be subject to increase if rises in costs necessitate

LAWERS. Machuim Farmhouse, Lawers, Aberfeldy. Sleeps 7 plus cot. Charming detached farmhouse; fully modernised, spacious and tastefully decorated. Superb location on lower slopes of Ben Lawers provides magnificent views of Loch Tay and surrounding hills. Three bedrooms (one en-suite). Downstairs bathroom with shower; very well equipped, newly fitted kitchen, automatic washing machine; comfortable lounge with TV and open fireplace. Total electric heating throughout. Fenced garden and ample parking. Bed linen and towels not provided. Walking, climbing, touring, fishing, horse riding, golf and water sports centre nearby. Hotel within walking distance. Rates from £175 to £325 weekly including electricity. Contact: **Mr and Mrs J.H. Webb (0283 840498).**

LAWERS (Aberfeldy). Shian Cottage, Lawers, By Aberfeldy. Sleeps 4 plus cot. Detached cottage on side of Loch Tay. Secluded close to burn with waterfalls. One room with double bed, one room with full size bunk beds, bathroom upstairs. Well equipped with night storage heaters, log burner in lounge area. Electric cooker, fridge, microwave, kettle, toaster, colour TV. Bed linen and towels not provided. Ideal for touring, walking, climbing, fishing, golf, horse riding and all water sports. Hotel within walking distance, Aberfeldy, Pitlochry, the Trossachs, Callander, Killin within easy reach. Rates £145 to £250 per week, electricity included, no VAT. Details from **Mr and Mrs J.H. Webb, Hurst Farm, Bromley Hurst, Abbots Bromley, Near Rugeley, Staffordshire WS15 3AP (0283 840498).**

LOCH RANNOCH. This is a small family property set amidst birch and pine forests on the south shore of Loch Rannoch, in the heart of the Perthshire Highlands. Traditional stone cottage, with modern well-equipped kitchen and bathroom, provides warm and comfortable self-catering accommodation. The scenery is magnificent. A wide variety of countryside — mountain, moor and forest, marsh, river and loch — is within walking distance. Much reduced rents are available in the Spring and Autumn, which are particularly attractive times for a holiday at Rannoch. Magnificent scenery, fascinating walks, bird watching, trout fishing, a warm fire to return to, peaceful surroundings. **Mr Reddish, 11 Lilybank Place, Aberdeen AB2 3PX (0224 481309).**

  See also Colour Display Advertisement **METHVEN. Mr H. England, Strathearn Holidays, Dept F93, Freepost, Kilda Way, Muirton Industrial Estate, Perth PH1 3RL (Office [0738] 33322 or Evenings [0738] 840263).** 🏵🏵🏵 *Highly Commended.* Cottages ideally situated in the centre of 650 acres of arable farm all enjoying lovely views. Sporting and leisure activities include golf, shooting, fishing, riding; touring castles, palaces and historic houses; easy access to the Highlands, Edinburgh and Glasgow. Send for our 12 page colour brochure (no stamp required).

WELCOME!

Country Houses and Cottages, sleeping 2/15, available in

PERTHSHIRE, THE HIGHLANDS & WEST OF SCOTLAND

Within easy reach you will find a fascinating variety of GOLF COURSES to play;
LOCHS and RIVERS to fish; HILLS and GLENS to explore.

For further information and for our FREE Brochure please write or telephone:

BELL-INGRAM

DURN, ISLA ROAD, PERTH PH2 7HF. TEL: 0738 21121 (24 HOURS)

See also Colour Display Advertisement PITLOCHRY. Mrs MacIntyre, Dunalastair Holiday Houses, 1 Riverside, Tummel Bridge, Pitlochry PH16 5SB (0882 634285). Up to ♥♥♥♥ *Commended.* The cottages are situated amongst and with views of some of the most beautiful scenery in Scotland. Ideal for hill walking, climbing and bird watching. Golf within half an hour. Excellent brown trout fishing, use of boats rent free. Accommodation for four/eight, all electric and open fire in livingroom. Off peak heating Spring/Autumn. Dunalastair is a National Scenic Area and is in a perfect central position from which to tour Scotland. Rates from £126 to £370, including VAT, weekly. Available March to November. Weekends negotiable. Send large SAE for details.

STRATHTAY. Carnish, Strathtay. Sleeps 4. Modern semi-detached bungalow, comfortably furnished, on edge of small village. Aberfeldy five miles, Pitlochry nine miles; near golf course. Sleeps four in two double bedrooms; electric blankets; fully equipped except linen; fridge; all-electric; parking. No children, no pets. Weekly terms plus electricity. Mrs Kidd, Eiriostadh, Strathtay, Pitlochry PH9 0PG (Strathtay [0887] 840322).

RENFREWSHIRE

BISHOPTON. The East Gatelodge, Formakin Estate, Mill Hill Road, Bishopton PA7 5NX (0505 863400). ♥♥♥♥ Sleeps 2/4. The East Gatelodge is situated in the grounds of Formakin Estate. It comprises bathroom, kitchen, lounge and bedroom. Colour TV, central heating; linen supplied. Terms range from £210 to £250 per week depending on season. Weekend breaks (Friday 5pm to Monday 9.30am) £120. Car parking. Garden. Snack bar/coffee shop. Laundry and ironing facilities. Groceries may be ordered in advance. Formakin is renowned as an architectural gem, designed by Lorimer, and is famous for its gardens. Much to see and do in the area. For further details please telephone or write.

ROSS-SHIRE

GAIRLOCH. Glendale House (FHG), South Erradale, Gairloch IV21 2AT (0445 83 206 or 285). The

Glendale is a comfortable family-run establishment. The
accommodation comprises five self catering flats sleeping
four/six people with the use of lounge and bar facilities in the
evenings. The house is situated in a crofting township amid
some of the most beautiful scenery of Wester Ross and
makes a comfortable base for a touring holiday. Nearby there
is an excellent nine-hole golf course, also fishing, canoeing
and many safe sandy beaches with truly spectacular views.
Children welcome. Rates from £130.

GAIRLOCH. Mrs L. McKenzie, 16 Strath, Gairloch IV21 2BX (0445 2230). One house comprising

three bedrooms — two double, one treble; lounge/dining
room; kitchen; bathroom with bath and shower, and sun
lounge. One bungalow comprising double bedroom, bathroom with shower, kitchen and lounge. Both have electric
heating throughout, electric blankets and bed linen supplied,
automatic washing machine, fridge/freezer, colour TV. Both
properties situated on top of hill overlooking the loch with
panoramic views of Isle of Skye and Torridons; five minutes'
walk to village. The area has several beaches, golf course,
loch, sea and river fishing and scenic walks. Open January to
December. Price £120 to £170 per week.

GLENELG. Mr and Mrs Lamont, Creagmhor, Glenelg IV40 8LA (059982 231). We have a modern

bungalow (👑👑👑 Approved) and five chalets, also a
modern caravan with all facilities, in an area unsurpassed for
sheer grandeur and magnificence. Over eight miles of dramatic but good single track road from the A87, 25 miles Kyle.
Superb area for the peaceful outdoor life and many sites of
historic interest. Local sea fishing is good with boats available for hire. Sandy beach and splendid coastline nearby.
Children and pets welcome. Write or phone for terms.

**LOCHCARRON. The Cottage, Stromecarronach, Lochcarron West, Strathcarron. Working farm,
join in. Sleeps 2.** The small, stone-built Highland cottage is fully equipped and has a double bedroom,
shower room and open plan kitchen/livingroom (with open fire). It is secluded with panoramic views over
Loch Carron and the mountains. River, sea and loch fishing are available. Hill walking is popular in the area,
and there is a small local golf course. Nearby the Isle of Skye, Inverewe Gardens, the Torridon and
Applecross Hills and the historic Kyle Railway Line. Visitors' dogs are welcome provided they are kept under
control at all times. For full particulars, write or telephone **Mrs A.G. Mackenzie, Stromecarronach,
Lochcarron West, Strathcarron IV54 8YH (Lochcarron [052-02] 284).**

ULLAPOOL. Mrs J. Renwick, Clachan, Lochbroom, Ullapool IV23 2RZ (0854 85209). Come and
relax in the tranquillity of Lochbroom in two modern three-bedroomed croft bungalows. They are in an
elevated position overlooking Lochbroom, 12 miles from Ullapool and 50 miles north of Inverness. Fully
equipped kitchen, very comfortably furnished, they are all electric with card meter. The comfort of guests is
our main priority. Central for touring. In easy reach of Corrieshellach Gorge, Inverewe Botanical Gardens,
Achiltibuie Hydroponicum and Knockan Nature Reserve. Linen extra if required. No smoking. No Sunday
enquiries.

HIGHLAND REGION – AND THE ISLANDS TOO!
From the genteel town of Inverness to the ragged formations of the west-coast and
on, over the sea to Skye and many more islands – yes Highland Region is vast!
You'll probably not find that many people but places that most definitely should be
found include, the Caledonian Canal, Culloden, Mallaig, Loch Ness, Inverewe,
Duncansby Head, Ben Nevis, the Cairngorms, Golspie, and the Islands themselves.

ROXBURGHSHIRE

DENHOLM. Mrs Philippa McCarter, Dykes Farm, Denholm, Hawick TD9 8TB (045087 323). Sleeps 4.

Delightful semi-detached cottage on farm in lovely countryside with wonderful views. Ideal for families or couples touring Scottish Borders and Northumberland and for walking, golf, fishing, riding. Denholm village two miles, easy reach of Hawick, Jedburgh, Kelso and the Cheviot Hills; Edinburgh approximately one and a quarter hours. This warm, comfortable cottage has livingroom with open fire (some fuel supplied), TV. Two bedrooms (one double and one twin), kitchen (electric cooker, fridge, washing machine), bathroom. Small garden, parking and garage. Linen supplied. Cot or Z-bed. Home cooked food from farmhouse available. Metered electricity. Well behaved dogs welcome (maximum two). Weekly terms from £90.

JEDBURGH. Mrs D. Tweedie, Buchtrig, Hownam, Jedburgh TD8 6NJ (083-54 230). This attractive detached, stone-built, whitewashed cottage has a superb position on a hill farm in the Cheviot Hills. Ideal for walking, but within easy reach of Border towns, Abbeys and sporting facilities. The cottage stands in its own enclosed well-kept garden and consists of a sitting/diningroom with a log/coal fire, colour TV. Two double bedrooms. Bathroom. Immersion heater. Kitchen with modern electric cooker and family size fridge. All rooms are well furnished and have fitted carpets. There are three night storage heaters, plus two electric fires. Ample parking space. Pets by request. Jedburgh 10 miles. Available May to October. Brochure.

KELSO. Mr and Mrs Archie Stewart, Clifton Hill, Kelso TD5 7QE (0573 225028). Crags Cottage,

renovated 1991 to a high standard yet maintaining its character and charm. It is situated on a working farm surrounded by beautiful Scottish Border countryside. Ideal base for touring the Borders — Abbeys, Floors Castle, Mellerstain House, Marderston. Kelso two miles, Berwick 18 miles, Edinburgh 35 miles. Craggs Cottage sleeps six in one luxurious double room and two twin rooms (one large and one very small). Spacious kitchen with Rayburn cooker, washing machine. Cosy sittingroom with log fire. Garden with garden furniture and barbecue. Excellent restaurant nearby. Brochure on request. Sorry, no pets. Terms from £60 to £300; three-day Winter Breaks £60. Also available Clematis and Rose Cottages — terraced farm cottages making ideal two-family holidays — fully furnished with neat gardens. Small river for fishing, paddling or relaxing. Bed and Breakfast available at farmhouse. Phone or write for brochure.

NEWCASTLETON. The Roughley Cottage, Shaws Farm, Newcastleton. Working farm. Sleeps 5.

This exceptional cottage is only three-quarters of an hour from the M6 at Carlisle. 1000 ft. up in the middle of a sheep farm, it has superb views of Hermitage Castle, beautiful and historic Liddesdale and the distant Lake District. It has great charm and originality combined with modern comfort. There are two single and one double bedrooms with extra bed and cot. Bathroom. Sitting/diningroom with open fire. Kitchen, larder, gas cooker, fridge, lighting and heating. Large barn. Fishing is available in well-stocked trout loch within casting distance of the front door. Pick your own fruit in season from the cottage garden. The Roughley is an ideal base for walking, bird watching and exploring the lovely Scottish Borders. Newcastleton, six miles away, has restaurants, shops, pubs, etc. For details telephone or write **T.W. and Lady E. Tennant, Shaws Farm, Newcastleton TD9 0SH (Steele Road [03873] 76241).**

YETHOLM. Mrs Freeland-Cook, Cliftoncote Farm, Yetholm, Kelso TD5 8PU (057382 241). Working farm, join in. Sleep 4/7. Terraced Cottages on typical Borders sheep farm (1052 acres). Peaceful rural setting, comfortable, homely, clean and well equipped. Splendid views and friendly atmosphere. Ideal hill walking (end of Pennine Way) and touring base, Border Abbeys and mills close by. Coast and Northumberland only half an hour; Edinburgh one hour. Golf, fishing, pony trekking available. Open fire (logs supplied), electricity by meter reading, parking, colour TV, twin tub washing machine, garden and play area. Cots, high chairs, etc. Sorry no dogs (lots of our own). Weekly rates £75 low season, £125/£150 high season. A warm welcome awaits you. Bed and Breakfast also available at farmhouse for extra visitors.

PLEASE SEND A STAMPED ADDRESSED ENVELOPE WITH ENQUIRIES

SUTHERLAND

LAIRG. Mrs Joan MacDonald, Builnatobrach Farm Cottages, Lairg IV27 4DB (0549 2235/2282). ❀❀❀/❀❀❀❀ *Commended.* Situated on a hillside overlooking Lairg and Loch Shin, Builnatobrach Farm Cottages provide quality accommodation, with beautiful scenery. Lairg and the surrounding area have many activities to offer — golf, fishing, hill walking, bird watching, tennis are easily available. Lairg being just one hour's drive north of Inverness is also an ideal touring base for Caithness, Sutherland and Ross-shire. The cottages sleeping four/six or eight are all fully equipped including microwave ovens. Each cottage has an open fire as well as electric central heating. Linen and coal can be supplied if required. Terms from £100 to £320 per week.

WIGTOWNSHIRE

NEWTON STEWART. Mrs Mary F. Hay, Shore Cottage, Alticry, Port William, Newton Stewart DG8 9RT (05815 278). Sleeps 2. Self-contained wing of country cottage situated on the shores of Luce Bay — 200 yards from the sea — six miles north-west of Port William. Fully equipped modern kitchen; shower room with toilet; colour TV in lounge. Bed linen supplied. Electricity, central heating and hot water included (no hidden extras). Tariff for this year is £85 to £95 per week. The area enjoys a mild climate due to the Gulf Stream. Ideally suited for exploring Galloway, which has great historical and archaeological interest. Inland the Galloway hills offer walking and driving through spectacular scenery. Many safe beaches. Golf, tennis, pony trekking; sea, river and loch fishing available. Several gardens open to the public. Pets permitted. Car essential — parking. Open all year. No smoking, please.

See also Colour Display Advertisement **NEWTON STEWART. Conifers Leisure Park, Kirroughtree, Newton Stewart DG8 6AN (Newton Stewart [0671] 2107).** Twenty-nine self-catering, luxury, furnished chalets, sleep four/six persons and attractively set amidst pine woods. Colour TV. All electric. Two saunas and solarium on site. FREE salmon and sea trout fishing and FREE golf to our visitors. Tennis court and barbecue area, heated pool. Tour the beautiful countryside. For the sportsman — river, loch and sea angling, riding, shooting, all within easy reach. A privately owned hotel adjacent, a nine-hole golf course close by. Open all year. Brochure and details on request.

2, Old Bank Chambers, Station Road, Horley, Surrey RH6 9HW
Tel: 0293 774535   Fax: 0293 784647   Minicom: 0293 776943

Holiday Care Service is a national charity which provides free holiday information and support to disabled people, elderly or singles, one parent families, people on low income and carers. We produce regional accessible accommodation guides for the UK, and information on many aspects of taking a holiday. We also provide a consultancy service to the industry.

We will help anyone who asks!

The famous 'Queen's View' of
Loch Tummel in Perthshire,
with the cone of Schiehallion
to the left of the picture.

CARAVAN AND CAMPING HOLIDAYS

ARGYLL

CARAVANS

 ## APPIN HOLIDAY CARAVANS
Truly magnificent setting right on the Lochside

8 very private caravans. All recent models, each fully serviced.
Laundrette, recreation room, play area and babysitting.
FREE fishing (salt and freshwater). Boating and sailing, great hill walks.
Pony trekking and Licensed Inn nearby.
Special Spring and Autumn terms. Price Guide – £135 to £235 per unit weekly.

Please send SAE for colour brochure giving dates required.

 **Mr & Mrs F.G. Weir, Appin Holiday Caravans, Appin,
Argyll PA38 4BQ   Telephone: Appin 287 (063173-287)**

For more details, see our advert in the colour section of this guide.

DALMALLY by. Mr and Mrs E. Crawford, Blarghour Farm, Lochawe-side, By Dalmally PA33 1BW (Kilchrenan [086-63] 246). A holiday caravan close to Loch Awe with views of the loch and forest-clad hills. Sleeping up to eight in two double and four single berths, fully equipped with continental quilts and pillows — linen on request. The caravan is 28' long, open plan living area with separate double and bunk bedrooms. Lounge with electric fire and colour TV. Kitchen with electric cooker, fridge, toaster and kettle, H/C. Bathroom with shower and flush toilet, H/C. Laundry facilities. Sorry, no pets. Fishing, boating, walking. Brochure on request. Please see colour advertisement on page 000.

AYRSHIRE

CARAVANS

SKELMORLIE. Mains Caravan and Camping Park, Skelmorlie Mains Farm, Skelmorlie PA17 5EU (0475 520794). The Park is situated just south of Skelmorlie on the hill overlooking the Firth of Clyde behind Skelmorlie Castle, half a mile above the main A78, within a working farm. Largs four miles, Wemyss Bay two miles. Skelmorlie is centrally placed for ferries to the Islands, as a halt on your journey north or south and as a base for discovering the West Coast of Scotland. Accommodation available includes modern six-berth caravans with gas cooking and heating, electricity, mains water and flush toilets; tourers welcome within main static park, hard standing or grass pitches with or without electricity; grass area with access road in separate area for tents. Also available, first floor flat with sittingroom, two bedrooms (sleeps six), kitchen, own garden entrance, parking and use of bathroom and shower. Full information and terms available on request.

INVERNESS-SHIRE

CARAVANS

ARISAIG. Mr A.A. Gillies, Kinloid Farm, Arisaig PH39 4NS (068-75 366). Working farm. Caravans sleep 6. Eight caravans (six berth) available for hire from Easter to October. Attractively situated occupying an elevated position at Kinloid Farm, a five-minute car run from wonderful sands. The caravans are new models and have hot and cold water, showers, fridges, electric lighting, flush toilets and are completely self-contained. Each van commands magnificent and extensive views across Arisaig to the sea and islands of Skye, Rhum and Eigg. Sea cruises from Arisaig to the Islands. Toilet block with hot and cold showers, washbasins, shaver points, laundry rooms. Shops in Arisaig village. Children welcome. Well-behaved pets are allowed. Weekly terms from £120. Huge reductions early/late season. SAE, please. Tourist Board registered.

FORT WILLIAM. Mr J. Fraser, Cross Cottage, North Ballachulish, Onich, Fort William PH33 6RZ (Onich [08553] 335). This small caravan site lies on the "Druim" which skirts the eastern shores of Onich Bay. Surrounded by the majestic crests of the Glencoe and Ardgour mountains, the site is an ideal centre for touring much of the Western Highlands. Eight modern caravans, all large six-berths (25ft — 34ft) have mains water, electric light, fridge, gas cooker and fire, colour TV. All have flush toilet; hot and cold water, washbasin and shower. Laundry facilities. Children welcome and they may bring their pets. Post Office and shops within two miles. Shingle beach 200 yards. Boats for hire, hill walking, forest trails, fishing etc. Visit many places of historic and scenic beauty. Every help given to enjoy your holiday. Weekly rates from £120 to £233. SAE, please, for further details. Available from January to December.

FORT WILLIAM. Mrs Margaret Dewar, Cuilcheanna House, Onich, Fort William PH33 6SD (Onich

[085-53] 226). The nine caravans for hire are pleasantly situated adjacent to the hotel within about one-and-a-half acres of ground, with plenty of space for children. The site is a quarter-mile off the main A82 and nine miles from Fort William. Most caravans are six-berth and include three 1988/89 models, approximately 30 feet long and complete with own shower and toilet, hot and cold, fridge, TV, gas cooking, heating and electricity. They are fully equipped except linen. Site facilities include laundry room, pay phone. Bar suppers in nearby licensed hotel. Post Office and shopping within one mile, the sea 250 yards away. Children welcome and one pet per family. Open Easter to late October. Weekly rates £95 to £230 inclusive. Further details on application. Tourist Board Registered.

SPEAN BRIDGE. Mrs M.H. Cairns, Invergloy House, Spean Bridge PH34 4DY (Spean Bridge

[039-781] 681; from Summer 1993 [0397] 712681). Caravans sleep 5. Two luxury caravans (one 29ft with double bedroom, double berth and one single berth, the other 31ft with double bedroom, twin/double second bedroom, single berth). Each caravan is secluded from the other with natural woodland. Shower, toilet and washbasin, Calor gas cooking and heating, electric lighting and fridge provided in each caravan. All fully equipped except linen. Situated in beautiful secluded grounds of 50 acres overlooking Loch Lochy. Private shingle beach reached by footpath. Free fishing, rowing boats for hire, use of hard tennis court. Spean Bridge (five miles) has supermarket. Fort William 15 miles. Golf and pony trekking nearby. Ideal place to explore Highlands, Loch Ness, Glencoe, Skye; sport at Aviemore Centre. Children welcome. Controlled dog accepted. Open from 1st April to 31st October. Weekly terms from £160 to £215. £10 discount when only two occupants. Daily letting out of high season. Ideal for "gentle holiday in peaceful surroundings". SAE, please, for further details. Tourist Board registered.

ROSS-SHIRE

CARAVANS

POOLEWE. Mrs Jeanne Munro, Spring Cottage, 3 Coast, Inverasdale, Achnasheen, Poolewe IV22 2VR (0445 86 438). Situated in this picturesque area of Wester Ross in the Highland region of Scotland, this modern residential caravan is near the shores overlooking a beautiful sandy beach with views up Loch Ewe to the world famous Inverewe Gardens and the mountains beyond. The two bedroomed caravan has electricity for lights, fridge, TV, washer, etc., and gas for cooking, hot water, heating and shower. The area is ideal for people who love hill walking, loch and sea fishing, boating or just exploring this wonderful countryside. Children welcome. Terms from £95 to £175 per week.

WIGTOWNSHIRE

CARAVANS

PORT WILLIAM. Auchness Caravan Park, Port William. Mobile homes, on Auchness Caravan Park, just off B7021, consisting of three bedrooms, bathroom with flush toilet, washbasin and shower, full gas cooker, fire and water heater, electric lights, fridge and TV. Vans fully equipped including linen and cutlery. Gas and electricity provided. Play area for small children and access to private swimming pool. Pony trekking nearby and bowls, tennis, fishing are available at Port William and Whithorn/Isle of Whithorn, also golf course at Monreith where there are safe sandy beaches. From £90 per week. Also historic dig at Whithorn where St. Ninian established the first church in this area. Some brand new mobile homes available. Please apply to: **Mrs E. Walker, Barwinnock Farm, Whauphill, Port William DG8 9PX (Port William [098-87] 291).**

ACTIVITY
HOLIDAYS

See also Colour Display Advertisement **HIGHLANDS.** Discover a true piece of the Highlands and Islands for yourself. There's no place like the Highlands and Islands of Scotland in Spring and Summer. It's a land steeped in history and rich with visual splendour. Whole hillsides burst into bright colours. Long golden sunsets go right on till dawn. And to cap it all there's our legendary Highland hospitality. It's a land you'll find easy to discover, too, thanks to our 148 page Spring/Summer brochure. It's packed with holiday ideas, with a wealth of activities for every age group. So come and enjoy a holiday you'll never forget — in the Highlands and Islands of Scotland. For your colour brochure call free on **0800 838 166** or write to: **Highlands and Islands of Scotland, Freepost (AD5), Inverness IV1 1BY.**

See also Colour Display Advertisement **PEEBLESSHIRE, WEST LINTON. Mrs C.M. Kilpatrick, Slipper-field House, West Linton EH46 7AA (West Linton [0968] 60401).** 🏵🏵🏵/🏵🏵🏵🏵 *Commended.* **Properties sleep 4/6.** Two Commended cottages a mile from West Linton at foot of Pentland Hills, set in 100 acres of lochs and woodlands. **AMERICA COTTAGE** sleeps six in three bedrooms, is secluded and has recently been completely modernised. Equipment includes washing machine, dryer, microwave oven and telephone. **LOCH COTTAGE** sleeps four in two bedrooms, is attached to owner's house, and has magnificent views over a seven acre loch. Both cottages have sittingroom with dining area and colour TV; modern bathrooms; excellently equipped Schreiber kitchens. Controlled pets allowed. Car essential — ample parking. Golf and private fishing. Available all year. Edinburgh 19 miles. SAE for terms.

FOR THE MUTUAL GUIDANCE
OF GUEST AND HOST

Every year literally thousands of holidays, short-breaks and overnight stops are arranged through our guides, the vast majority without any problems at all. In a handful of cases, however, difficulties do arise about bookings, which often could have been prevented from the outset.

It is important to remember that when accommodation has been booked, both parties — guests and hosts — have entered into a form of contract. We hope that the following points will provide helpful guidance.

GUESTS: When enquiring about accommodation, be as precise as possible. Give exact dates, numbers in your party and the ages of any children. State the number and type of rooms wanted and also what catering you require — bed and breakfast, full board, etc. Make sure that the position about evening meals is clear — and about pets, reductions for children or any other special points.

Read our reviews carefully to ensure that the proprietors you are going to contact can supply what you want. Ask for a letter confirming all arrangements, if possible.

If you have to cancel, do so as soon as possible. Proprietors do have the right to retain deposits and under certain circumstances to charge for cancelled holidays if adequate notice is not given and they cannot re-let the accommodation.

HOSTS: Give details about your facilities and about any special conditions. Explain your deposit system clearly and arrangements for cancellations, charges, etc, and whether or not your terms include VAT.

If for any reason you are unable to fulfil an agreed booking without adequate notice, you may be under an obligation to arrange alternative suitable accommodation or to make some form of compensation.

While every effort is made to ensure accuracy, we regret that FHG Publications cannot accept responsibility for errors, omissions or misrepresentation in our entries or any consequences thereof. Prices in particular should be checked because we go to press early. We will follow up complaints but cannot act as arbiters or agents for either party.

ONE FOR YOUR FRIEND 1993

FHG Publications have a large range of attractive holiday accommodation guides for all kinds of holiday opportunities throughout Britain. They also make useful gifts at any time of year. Our guides are available in most bookshops and larger newsagents but we will be happy to post you a copy direct if you have any difficulty. We will also post abroad but have to charge separately for post or freight.

The inclusive cost of posting and packing the guides to you or your friends in the UK is as follows:

Farm Holiday Guide ENGLAND, WALES and IRELAND
Board, Self-catering, Caravans/Camping, Activity Holidays. Over 400 pages. **£4.00**

Farm Holiday Guide SCOTLAND
All kinds of holiday accommodation. **£3.00**

SELF-CATERING & FURNISHED HOLIDAYS
Over 1000 addresses throughout for Self-catering and caravans in Britain. **£3.50**

BRITAIN'S BEST HOLIDAYS
A quick-reference general guide for all kinds of holidays. **£3.00**

The FHG Guide to CARAVAN & CAMPING HOLIDAYS
Caravans for hire, sites and holiday parks and centres. **£3.00**

BED AND BREAKFAST STOPS
Over 1000 friendly and comfortable overnight stops. Non-smoking, The Disabled and Special Diets Supplements. **£3.50**

CHILDREN WELCOME! FAMILY HOLIDAY GUIDE
Family holidays with details of amenities for children and babies. **£4.00**

Recommended SHORT BREAK HOLIDAYS IN BRITAIN
'Approved' accommodation for quality bargain breaks. Introduced by John Carter. **£4.00**

Recommended COUNTRY HOTELS OF BRITAIN
Including Country Houses, for the discriminating. **£4.00**

Recommended WAYSIDE INNS OF BRITAIN
Pubs, Inns and small hotels. **£4.00**

PGA GOLF GUIDE
Where to play and where to stay
Over 2000 golf courses in Britain with convenient accommodation. Endorsed by the PGA. Holiday Golf in France, Portugal and Majorca. **£8.50**

PETS WELCOME!
The unique guide for holidays for pet owners and their pets. **£4.00**

BED AND BREAKFAST IN BRITAIN
Over 1000 choices for touring and holidays throughout Britain. Airports and Ferries Supplement. **£3.00**

THE FRENCH FARM AND VILLAGE HOLIDAY GUIDE
The official guide to self-catering holidays in the 'Gîtes de France'. **£8.50**

Tick your choice and send your order and payment to FHG PUBLICATIONS, ABBEY MILL BUSINESS CENTRE, SEEDHILL, PAISLEY PA1 1TJ (TEL: 041-887 0428. FAX: 041-889 7204). **Deduct** 10% for 2/3 titles or copies; 20% for 4 or more.

Send to: NAME ....

ADDRESS ....

....

.... POST CODE ....

I enclose Cheque/Postal Order for £ ....

SIGNATURE .... DATE ....